PRAISE FOR

But Definitely Wear Mascara

"Nikki brings sparkle to everything she does, and this book is no exception. She conveys real life lessons through her fun, storytelling style and encourages you in a way that feels like a warm hug from an old friend. You'll feel her love for other moms springing off of every page."

—**Susie Moore**, Host of the *Let It Be Easy* podcast

"Nikki Oden walks the walk. Every truth-bomb and piece of advice in her book, *But Definitely Wear Mascara,* comes straight from her own experience. She normalizes the tough parts of motherhood to help you realize you're not alone. Her gritty, resilient spirit will inspire you to take action to create a mom life you love."

—**Ruth Soukup**, mother of two, *New York Times* best-selling author of *Living Well Spending Less: 12 Secrets of the Good Life*

"Nikki Oden is that supportive, straight-talking mom friend we all crave, the one who will always tell you when you have spinach in your teeth simply because she cares about you. Through her hilarious, easy-to-read stories, Nikki offers tangible advice that will make your mom life easier. This book is a must-read for all moms who are simultaneously nurturing their families and their careers."

—**Farnoosh Torabi**, mother of two, editor-at-large of CNET Money and host of the *So Money* podcast

"*But Definitely Wear Mascara* is as charming and helpful as Nikki herself. An easy read full of meaningful lessons, this book will have you laughing out loud (maybe sometimes at yourself) and reflecting on your life choices with honesty and humor. Nikki is full of brilliant, accessible advice that all women need in their life."

—Jamie Jensen, award-winning writer, creative business coach, and host of the *Creatives Making Money* podcast

"Nikki is like the mom best friend you didn't know you needed. She'll walk you through how to tackle mom life with grace and humor but isn't afraid to dole out the tough love when you need it. If you're a mom, you need this book."

—Cameron Normand, stepmom of four, owner of This Custom Life, co-owner/co-CEO of *Stepfamily Magazine*, and host of *The Stepmom Diaries* podcast

"This book is an absolute gem! In her unique, hilarious, and straight-to-the point manner, Nikki tells stories that are so relatable and will touch the hearts of moms around the world. Nikki's gorgeous, bubbly personality shines through in everything she does, and this book is no exception. You won't be able to put it down!"

—Jo Dodd, mother of four, best-selling author and coach, and author of *Dear Mama Bear with the F*cked Up Hair*

"Reading Nikki's book is like talking with a good girlfriend. You can feel her passion in every word. Nikki is genuine and funny! You will find yourself leaning in to soak up all she shares. She gets what it means to be a working mom with dreams and goals trying to rock it all. She will keep you engaged and you will have a blast as you learn how to love your mom life a little more!"

—Yamiek Anthony, mother of two, supporter of working moms, and founder of Rockstar Career Moms

"Nikki Oden is the outlet you have been searching for, who just gets it and helps you get things done with more joy, more clarity, and better perspective."

—Nellie Harden, mother of four, founder of The 6570 Family Project and creator of the Take The Lead program

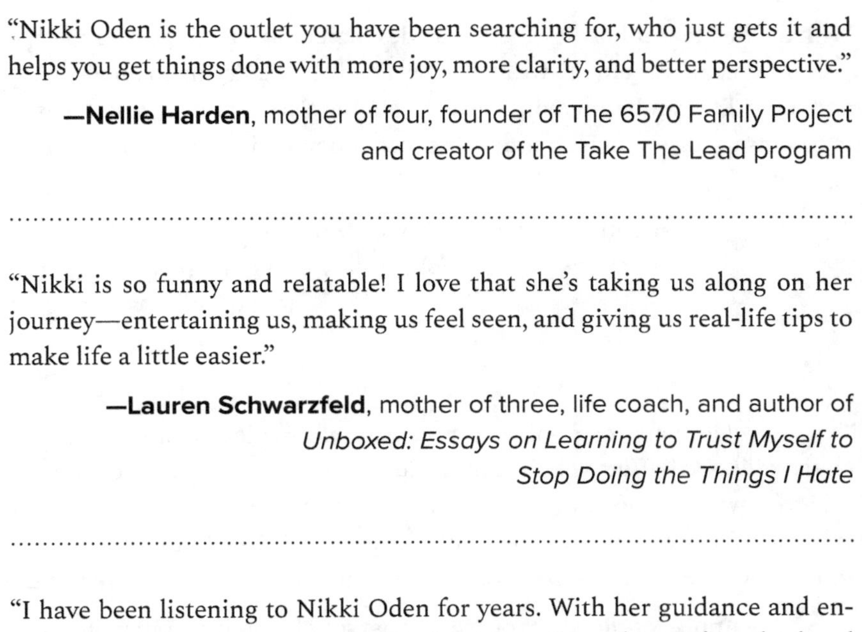

"Nikki is so funny and relatable! I love that she's taking us along on her journey—entertaining us, making us feel seen, and giving us real-life tips to make life a little easier."

—Lauren Schwarzfeld, mother of three, life coach, and author of *Unboxed: Essays on Learning to Trust Myself to Stop Doing the Things I Hate*

"I have been listening to Nikki Oden for years. With her guidance and encouragement, my journey to finding happiness in and out of motherhood has been inspiring. Reading Nikki's story about getting out of her motherhood rut and finding herself again really resonated with me and has given me that push to find myself again. Nikki is real, vulnerable, and authentic. This book is a must for any mama trying to find herself again and figure out 'what's next.'"

—Kendahl Yanez, mother of two, founder and host of the *Mama, You're Doing Great!* podcast

"Nikki is as down-to-earth as you can get. She is a real person who truly embraces being a mom, while at the same time showing us it's not all roses and champagne. Nikki talks about the hard things, teaches us how to give ourselves grace, and walks the walk. This book is a must-read for moms everywhere."

—Kristy Baranovskis, mother of two, Kitchen Confidence Coach, founder of Kitchen Confidence

"Nikki Oden tells it how it is. She provides incredible insight, tips, and support for the crazy mom life we all live on a daily basis. Trying to juggle work and mom life can be incredibly overwhelming. Nikki creates a safe space for moms to regain their confidence. I recommend this book to all my mom clients."

—**Leeann Rybakov**, mother of two and health coach to busy, overwhelmed moms ready to regain their energy and feel good in their bodies

"Nikki provides approachable and practical information on a topic that is rarely addressed effectively in the world of goal achievement: how do we achieve anything among the inconsistent routines, competing priorities, and exhaustion in the joyful experience of motherhood? Nikki's insight and passion is always truly rewarding to experience, and this book is no exception."

—**Annie Mudin**, mother of one, personal development writer and speaker, and creator of www.sharinghangover.com

But
Definitely
Wear
Mascara

But Definitely Wear Mascara

HACKS TO HELP YOU LOVE YOUR MOM LIFE (AND YOURSELF) A LITTLE MORE

NIKKI ODEN

PHOENIX
ADVANTAGE MEDIA

Boynton Beach, Florida

BUT DEFINITELY WEAR MASCARA
Hacks to Help You Love Your Mom Life (and Yourself) a Little More

© 2023 Nicole Oden
All rights reserved.

Published by:
Phoenix Advantage Media
Boynton Beach, Florida

No part of this book may be reproduced or transmitted in any form or by any means, electronic or mechanical, including but not limited to: photocopying, recording, or by any information storage retrieval system without the written permission of the publisher, except for the inclusion of brief quotations in a review.

Limit of Liability/Disclaimer of Warranty: While the publisher and author have used their best efforts in preparing this book, they make no representations or warranties with respect to the accuracy or completeness of the contents of this book and specifically disclaim any implied warranties of merchantability or fitness for a particular purpose. No warranty may be created or extended by sales representatives or a written sales manual. The advice and strategies contained herein may not be suitable for your situation. You should consult with a professional where appropriate. Neither the publisher nor the author shall be liable for any loss of profit or any other commercial damages, including but not limited to special, incidental, consequential, or other damages. Additionally, the names in some of the stories contained in this book have been changed at the author's discretion or the participants' request.

Printed in the United States of America.

Editing: Cindy Cowherd
Editing: Clarisa Marcee, Avenue C Media
Cover Design & Interior Layout: Kendra Cagle (www.5LakesDesign.com)

Library of Congress Control Number: 2022922986

Publisher's Cataloging-in-Publication
(Provided by Cassidy Cataloguing Services, Inc.).

Names: Oden, Nikki, author.
Title: But definitely wear mascara : hacks to help you love your mom life (and yourself) a little more / Nikki Oden.
Description: Boynton Beach, Florida : Phoenix Advantage Media, [2023]
Identifiers: ISBN: 979-8-9871520-0-3 (paperback) | 979-8-9871520-1-0 (Kindle) | 979-8-9871520-2-7 (ePub)
Subjects: LCSH: Motherhood--Anecdotes. | Motherhood--Humor. | Work-life balance--Anecdotes. | Work-life balance--Humor. | Goal (Psychology)--Anecdotes. | Goal (Psychology)--Humor. | Self-esteem in women--Anecdotes. | Self-esteem in women--Humor. | LCGFT: Self-help publications. | Humor. | BISAC: FAMILY & RELATIONSHIPS / Parenting / Motherhood. | SELF-HELP / Self-Management / Time Management. | HUMOR / Topic / Marriage & Family.
Classification: LCC: HQ759 .O34 2023 | DDC: 306.8743/02--dc23

Nicole Oden
www.youridealmomlife.com
nikki@youridealmomlife.com

For Emma and Ryan

CONTENTS

INTRODUCTION

Hey there, girlfriend!

I'm not even going to try to play it cool. I'm *psyched* that you bought this book. If I could, I'd give you a hug to start things off, because I'm a major hugger.

Just like you, I'm juggling a lot of balls. I am a happy wife, a mother of two adorable (and rascally) kids, a Believer, a part-time lawyer, a mediocre tennis player, an aspiring sommelier (which is my classy way of saying I love wine), the founder and creator of Your Ideal Mom Life®, and the host of the *Love Your Mom Life* podcast.

It sounds like a lot, and it is—in the best way. And although I love my life today . . . that wasn't always the case.

See, much like the phoenix that bursts into flames, burns to ash, and rises to begin life again, I have fallen flat on my face and started over a thousand times.

When I was in high school, my family moved from Florida to Chile—a drastic change of scenery that kind of sucked at first. I spent the better part of six months feeling lost and friendless, which is a sixteen-year-old girl's worst nightmare. A year and a half later, I returned to the U.S. on my own as a freshman at Florida State University—go 'Noles!—and one day, while attempting to sell my plasma for extra spending money (*that's* a story best told over a glass of Chardonnay), I learned I have Type 1 Diabetes. Stunned, and with my parents in another hemisphere, I had to change my entire life and learn overnight how to manage a disease that still has no cure.

Later, after graduating college and working at my first real job, I met my first husband, who encouraged me to fulfill my dream of going to law school. Our marriage, however, was a total flop. After eighteen short months, we got divorced, and I felt humiliated, heartbroken, and like a complete failure.

Suffice it to say, if you feel like you're constantly falling on your face, or that you've had to start over again and again, I totally get it.

You are not alone.

In many ways, motherhood feels like a process of repeated starts, doesn't it?

After I married the love of my life and became a mom, I walked away from a lucrative career as a lawyer and settled into raising my children. In the beginning, I had two under two, and man did I fall on my face a lot. Aside from keeping my toddler from accidentally murdering my infant, I had no idea what I was doing, and most days, didn't brush my teeth. I completely lost myself in being "Mommy" and "Wife."

Eventually, I had to admit to myself that I wasn't happy. Like so many moms, I discovered I wanted to have an impact on the world outside of my family—but without forsaking them. It was through that process of trying to integrate *what* I wanted out of life as a woman with *who* I wanted to be as a mother (and dropping a lot of balls in the process) that I became passionate about helping other moms battle burnout, crush their goals, and lose the mom guilt. My deepest wish is for you to align with your highest and best self and refuse to be limited by self-doubt.

So wherever you are in your mom life right now, whether it's feeling like you're trying to be everything to everyone (and failing a little bit at everything in the process), dealing with constant mom guilt, struggling to make time for you without sacrificing time with your kids, or all of the above, I hear you. I've been there. And there is nothing wrong with you!

All moms struggle with harmonizing what they have to do with what they want to do, and it's OK to fall down along the way. As moms, we get back up and keep going. That's where our power comes from. I hope you'll join me in believing that everything you need to create the life of your dreams is already within you. You just have to harness it.

My mission is to help you love your mom life (and yourself) a little more.

That's why I wrote this book. Read it from start to finish, or in whatever order you want as the chapters speak to you.

As you're reading, just remember: you are fierce, passionate, and powerful beyond measure. And if you hang around me long enough, I'll make sure you believe it.

xo,

Nikki

Chapter One

YOUR MOM LIFE MANIFESTO

Before we dive in, I say we declare our intentions. I like to do this with a fancy schmancy thing called a *manifesto*. (Ahem. In case you didn't know, a "manifesto" is a written statement publicly declaring the intentions or views of its issuer. You probably did know, but I enjoy being thorough. I'm a nerd like that.)

Here's my mom life manifesto:

- I give myself **permission** to put my needs first.
- I choose to make time for **self-preservation** every day.
- I allow myself to **pursue** my biggest, hairiest, most audacious goals.
- I understand that I must **take care of myself** to be able to take care of my children and my family.
- I allow myself to **try new things** and choose to take the first step because I know the next step will reveal itself.

- I **refuse to be sidelined** by mom guilt.
- I give myself permission to **say no** to people and things that do not serve me.
- I **choose not to compare** myself to other moms.
- I choose to **surround myself** with people who are encouraging, supportive, and hold me accountable.
- I **give myself permission** to let go of perfectionism.
- I choose to **create harmony** over balance.
- I choose to **focus on quality** instead of quantity when I spend time with my children.
- I allow myself to **experience my emotions.**
- I am kind to myself when I fall down, and I choose to **get back up** and keep going.
- I give myself permission to **ask others for help.**
- I choose to **speak to myself** the way I would speak to someone I love.
- I believe that to love others more fully, I must first and foremost **love myself.**

Powerful, right?

I encourage you to think about what you truly want for your mom life and for yourself and adopt your own mom life manifesto.

Or if you like mine, just copy it. I won't tell anyone. Slap that baby on your bathroom mirror and start living it.

Chapter Two

THE THREE THINGS ALL MOMS
WHO ARE ROCKING IT KNOW

I used to feel like I was full of crap.

From the outside, it seemed like I was running a really successful business, that I was spending tons of quality time with my kids, and that I was giving my marriage the attention it deserved.

Truth?

I was working like a dog. If you think of work and life as two ends of a seesaw, my tush was planted firmly on the ground on the "work" side. There were a whole lot of trips to the park and museum I missed, lots of eating in the car (yes, while driving), and towering piles of dishes and laundry.that didn't get done.

I constantly felt spread thin. I wasn't taking care of myself. I felt like I was always letting someone down—on both sides of the seesaw. And don't even get me started on the mom guilt.

Do you ever feel that way, too?

It's OK, mama. I promise you, there is light at the end of that tunnel.

After a particularly crippling series of mom fails, I started making little changes. Slowly, in bite-sized chunks, and after a *lot* of trial and improvement, I figured out how to focus on what matters most in life, business, and motherhood. I got a grip on my time. I discovered how to be more of what I want to be and do more of what I want to do.

And I want that for you.

We're about to chat about what I learned (and continue to study every single day). But first, let's get real about why this stuff is even important.

Why your happiness matters.

Quite simply, it matters because **you** matter. You are the center of your household. And when you experience more presence, patience, and joy, that power will spill into everything you do.

Do you think your relationship with your kids would be better if you had more patience? Do you think your marriage would be more solid if you felt good about yourself?

Uh, the answer is yes, girlfriend. One hundred percent.

And obviously you want that, so let's get this party started.

First, stop lying to yourself.

Can we moms all band together and just get over the guilt thing?

For reals. Mom guilt is a lie we have been telling ourselves for so long we actually believe it. But does mom guilt make us better moms? Does it *fix* anything? Nope. Do you know what does?

Taking care of yourself.

You must make yourself a priority. Think about that universal safety training all airlines force flight attendants to perform for you during takeoff. You know—the one about what to do in "the unlikely event" the cabin loses pressure? What do they always tell you? Put *your* mask on first, *then* help others. Why?

If you aren't functioning at your highest and best, you can't show up for anyone else.

Refusing to make time for self-care because you've guilted yourself into believing that every waking moment of your life should be spent on everyone else first (your boss, your co-workers, your kids, your husband, your dog) is not serving you. You *will* eventually burn out, and you'll probably build up a whole bunch of resentment on your way there. In the airplane example, you might even faint. And then what good are you to anyone—especially your kids?

Remember, the only way to show up as the best version of you—whether you're parenting or nurturing your marriage or kicking ass at work—is to take care of yourself. Set aside time to do the things that fill you up.

Everyone you love deserves your best. Give it to them. Promote yourself to the top of your list and put your mask on first.

Second, set boundaries.

Let's get something straight right now.

Not everything matters equally. Stop acting like it does.

This piece of the puzzle is absolutely essential, my friend. If you find you're always saying yes to everything, even when you don't want to, start setting some boundaries right away. (Side note: it's no wonder you feel overwhelmed and spread thin!)

Look, I get it. In many ways, motherhood is an act of juggling. You're juggling the time you want to spend with your kiddos with the time you want to spend on yourself. You're juggling the time you devote to work or business with the time it takes to keep your house (somewhat) clean, your family (happily) fed, and your laundry (sort of) done. It can often feel as if you're throwing one ball high enough into the air to give yourself just enough time to catch another ball before it crashes to the ground.

This is where boundaries come in.

To set proper boundaries, you need to get crystal clear on your priorities. The best way I've seen this concept explained is in the game-changing, must-read book, *The One Thing*, by Gary Keller and Jay Papasan. Start by imagining that each major area of your life is a ball. Let's say your job or business is one ball (and if you have a job and a side hustle, each would be its own ball); your family is another ball; your friends and important relationships are another; your health is another; and your spirituality is yet another. If you have a hobby or a passion, like my love-hate relationship with tennis, that would be another ball.

The key to setting boundaries is understanding which balls are made of rubber and which are made of glass.

Your family, important relationships, health, and spirituality are glass balls. Re-read that sentence. I want you to fully wrap your mind around this concept.

If you drop a glass ball, it will shatter. Sure, you can try to glue it back together again, but the cracks will show. The adhesive will smear. The ball will never be the same. That's why you must set boundaries to protect the balls in your life that are made of glass.

A rubber ball, on the other hand, will always bounce when you drop it. *Work and business are rubber balls.* Yes, work is important because it allows us to feed and clothe our families, keep a roof over our heads, and enjoy certain luxuries. Your work may even be a huge passion of yours.

But is there only *one* way to make a living? Is there only one way to produce income? Nope. That's what makes work a rubber ball. While there are any number of jobs you might have in your lifetime, you only have one body and one soul. And your kids? Well . . . I don't need to tell you twice that there is absolutely no replacing them.

So if ever you're faced with having to drop a ball, drop the one that will bounce.

Within each "major" glass and rubber ball are smaller glass and rubber balls. For example, at work, there may be items you need to treat as glass balls if you don't want to get fired. On the flip side, with your family, there are plenty of items you can treat as rubber balls, like cooking every night or volunteering for the PTA bake sale. You get the idea. It all boils down to remembering that not everything matters equally and, when push comes to shove, remembering what matters *most*.

Once you're crystal clear on your priorities, setting boundaries that protect your glass balls becomes much easier. It also becomes a lot easier to see where we're lying to ourselves or selling ourselves short. Because the truth is, when we say, "I don't have time for that," what we're *really* saying is, "I choose not to make that a priority." Remember that the next time you're tempted to brush off self-care or something for you because you "don't have time" for it, and ask yourself if you're walking in alignment with your glass balls.

Now, if any of this boundary stuff sounds scary or overwhelming, remember that it's OK to start small. Begin with something simple, like setting a boundary around when you respond to texts, emails, and phone calls to ensure you're always present with your family at mealtime.

See? That wasn't so bad.

Third, speak to yourself the way you'd speak to someone you love.

Yeah, I know. It's easy to *say* you're going to make yourself a priority and it's easy to *say* you're going to set boundaries.

But when life happens and you wake up late or get slammed at work, aren't the promises you made to yourself the first you choose to ignore?

Yep. We've all been there.

So how do you actually keep them?

Well, you start by reminding yourself why all of this matters. Don't forget why it's important for you to make yourself a priority and why you need to protect your glass balls.

Then, as with any goal, you must start small. For example, you've probably gone the extra step of putting those promises you make to yourself in your calendar, or you've set alarms on your phone to remind yourself to go for a walk, or watch that tutorial you've had favorited on your list, or keep any number of other promises you've made to yourself. And then when the alarm goes off . . . you dismiss it. (Yeah, I see you!)

My recommendation? Make those calendar entries and alarms hard to ignore by changing the language you use for them. Instead of simply reminding yourself to "meditate" or "workout," use words that will be powerful for you. Speak to yourself the way you would speak to someone you love. My favorite phrase is, "Choose yourself right now and [fill in the blank with what I promised myself I'd do]." Another effective one is, "Hi beautiful!

Take some time right now to [fill in the blank with the promise you made to yourself]."

It sounds too simple to be effective, but I promise you, it works. The next time that alarm on your phone goes off, honor it. Remember that by keeping the promises you make to yourself, you are protecting a glass ball.

Losing the mom guilt, setting boundaries, and being nice to yourself might (probably will) happen slowly. But if you're intentional, it will happen. Just start small and don't stop. Remember why your happiness matters.

Chapter Three

GET OFF THE
HOT MESS EXPRESS

When you're a mom, it's easy to be a hot mess. Sometimes I feel like no one understands this ugly truth better than I do.

Although I've come a long way, I used to feel like every day was a game of whack-a-mole. I was constantly putting out fires and running from one thing to the next. I convinced myself I didn't have time to exercise or to do things that were just for me. Every week, a whole lot of tasks fell right through the cracks.

As I huffed and puffed through each day, I was baffled by the moms who seemingly always had time to exercise, serve their families home-cooked meals, volunteer, work, *and* straighten their hair. I wondered, *"How?* Do those fit, working, cooking, volunteering, smooth-haired women have time-turners from Dumbledore?"

I'll save you some research. The answer is no.

Eventually, after one mom fail too many, I made a decision. Something had to change in the way I was "managing" everything.

I realized that telling myself I didn't have time for something was nothing more than a lie. When we say we don't have time for something, what we're really saying is, "I choose not to make that a priority." It really is that simple. It's a *choice*.

Every mom—you, me, the mother in carline who is somehow *never* in her pajamas—has the exact same number of seconds, minutes, and hours to work with each day.

Once I understood that I get to decide what I make a priority in my life, I was able to take command of my schedule from a place of power, versus desperation. In bite-sized chunks, and after a lot of, "Well, *that* didn't work, let me try this," I went from overwhelmed to organized. I figured out how to create habits that help me focus on what matters most in life, help me be more of who I want to be, and do more of what I want to do.

Here's my best advice for getting off the Hot Mess Express and experiencing a more organized life.

Purge the mental clutter.

When your mind is cluttered with every single thing you need to do for every part of your multifaceted life, it's easy to feel crippled by overwhelm. That's why doing a regular mental dump is step number one in getting organized.

A mental dump is just what it sounds like: an active and intentional dump of everything that is in your head out onto paper. There is only one rule! A mental dump must be done in one place (read: do not do your mental dump on sticky notes!). Trust me, there's no point in doing a mental dump if parts of it are all over the place.

Now, when I say dump out "everything" that's in your head, I mean *everything*. Books you want to read. Courses you want to take. Drawers you want to organize. It doesn't matter what area of your life it pertains to, or how big or small it is. It doesn't matter if you think you'll never have time to do it. If it's on your mind, dump it onto the paper.

Despite being simple, this habit is incredibly powerful. It serves two purposes. First, it allows you to capture all of the little things that are swimming around in your head, making you feel overwhelmed, spread thin, and like you're one missed reminder away from dropping a ball (or five). Second, it promotes presence and tranquility. Getting organized is a heck of a lot easier when your mind isn't being pulled in thirty thousand directions.

Believe it to see it.

Once you've purged all that clutter from your mind, you'll have the capacity to visualize yourself getting organized.

The old adage goes, "I'll believe it when I see it," but in reality, it works the other way around. You have to believe it *first*, and *then* you'll see it materialize. And visualizing what you want your life to look like is the first step in believing it will eventually look that way.

So . . . what does your most amazing life look like?

Paint that picture in your mind. Give yourself permission to dive deep here. Envision every single detail.

Then, take it a step further and write those details in your journal or a Google doc, or simply send yourself an email. Personally, I'm a huge fan of vision boards. I don't do anything fancy, I just find images of what I'm envisioning on the internet, print them out, and paste those babies on a piece of poster board. Easy, and so effective.

When life gets hairy, as it often does when you're raising humans, come back to your visualization and remember why organizing your life matters to you.

Decide what you want to achieve in the next 12 months.

Seeing yourself living your best and most organized life is one thing. But how do you actually make it happen?

First, you have to decide exactly where you want to be one year from now, both personally and professionally. And you're gonna dream big. Like, really big. I'm in the "set-crazy-unrealistic-ginormous" goals camp. Trust me, despite what conventional goal-setting wisdom might tell you, setting huge goals is the way to go.

And don't waste one second worrying you might fall short. I promise, you will be far more fulfilled at the end of a year having missed a huge goal than you would be if you achieved a "realistic" goal. When it comes to goal setting, "realistic" is usually code for "minuscule." And you're not making all this effort to get organized just so you can do something small, are you?

Didn't think so.

What in your wildest dreams would you love to accomplish over the next year? Lose 100 pounds? Get promoted? Hit tennis balls like a pro? Open a cake store?

We're throwing fear out the window as you decide on your top personal and professional goals. Your only limit here is your own willingness to be big. Allow it. Big is awesome.

Take itty, bitty, teeny, tiny baby steps.

Once you have your big, hairy, audacious goals ("BHAGs" for short) crystallized in your mind, your next step is to determine what you need to do each day to make them happen.

Start with what you're going to have to accomplish on a monthly basis. What action step can you take each month that, if done consistently for 12 months, would result in you achieving each BHAG? Notice I said step, singular. You're simply deciding on one monthly milestone. So, for example, if your annual goal was to lose 100 pounds, your monthly milestone might be to lose 8 pounds.

But if you're going to stay focused (and off the Hot Mess Express), we've gotta trim it down even more. Once you've settled on your monthly milestone, the next step is to decide on one activity you can do this week to ensure you achieve your monthly milestone if you perform that activity for four straight weeks.

Often as you're answering this question, your first several responses will be milestones as well. Keep asking yourself the question until you get down to an activity. Using the weight-loss example, the weekly activity might be to walk five miles. (Side note: remember you're coming up with something you can do. There's no point in choosing something that sounds good but you know you won't actually do.)

Finally, whittle it down to the granular by asking yourself, "What's the one task I can do each day to ensure I complete my weekly activity?" Go as small as you can until you get down to a single task. In keeping with the weight-loss example, perhaps the task might be something as simple as, "Be in bed with face washed and teeth brushed by 9:30 PM," because that will ensure you wake up on time to go for your walk.

See where we're going with this? We're taking something big, hairy, and audacious and making it bite-sized.

Now, a word to all you perfectionists out there. It's OK if the activities and tasks you choose miss the mark at first. Do not let the fear of choosing the "wrong" task hold you back from even starting. If you end up being wrong about what your one thing is for each section, the beauty is that you'll figure it out quickly—and then you can adjust.

Sometimes knowing that you're doing the wrong thing can be more valuable than getting it right the first time. Just start and see what happens.

Prioritize and block it out.

Did reading that just make your brain hurt? Stay with me. I promise this habit isn't painful. Although "time blocking" sounds rigid and camp-counselor-clipboard-y, it's actually quite freeing.

After you've whittled your BHAGs down to bite-sized daily tasks, you'll block those items off on your calendar. Alternatively, if it's not something you would necessarily calendar, but lends itself well to an alarm or reminder, set those up in your phone.

My pro tip on setting reminders and calendar entries is to speak to yourself the way you would speak to someone you love.

Use language that will make those entries hard to ignore when they go off later and you're tempted to simply hit "Snooze" or "Dismiss." My go-to is, "Choose yourself right now and [do what you promised you'd do]." I'm also a fan of, "Remember why this matters and [do X]." Use words you know will be powerful for you.

Once you've blocked off time for your most important goals, you're already winning, because you're focusing on what matters most.

But . . . what about all that other stuff on your mental dump list?

This is where prioritizing comes in. To keep your life organized, you must accept that not all things on that list matter equally. The loud, urgent tasks are not always the most important, and the quick, easy ones are not necessarily what you should do first.

With that backdrop, read through your list, one item at a time. Next to each item, write an A, B, or C. "A" items are the ones you must do. "B" items are the ones you should do. "C" items are the ones you'd merely like to do. If you're more of a visual person, prioritize using three highlighters, where each color represents the "must do," "should do," and "would like to do" items.

When deciding on how to label the items on my list, I follow this rule: if it supports a BHAG in some way or counts as self-care, it's an "A" item, always. For everything else, go with your gut.

Next, get the "A" items on your calendar in the time slots that are left after you blocked your BHAG activities, then repeat the process for the "B" and "C" items. As you're blocking off your time, you might realize that some of your items are actually mislabeled (perhaps a couple of your As should really be Bs or vice versa). That's OK! You're in charge here. You get to revise the labels as needed.

Spoiler alert: not everything you wrote down during your mental dump is going to fit into one week.

But guess what? That's actually a good thing. The big benefit of having prioritized your to-dos is that only your most important items will make it onto the calendar. In other words? No more whack-a-mole!

You now have a place where your biggest goals are accounted for (your calendar) and a place where everything else is recorded (your mental dump sheet) so you can refer back to it if time slots open up.

Stop reacting.

This, my friend, is where stuff gets real. Anyone can *make* plans. But honoring them? That's an entirely different story.

I react way more often than I'd like to admit. I'll be sitting in my home office, serenely settling into the task I've blocked on my calendar for that precise moment, when—*squirrel!* My phone notifies me that I have a text. In that moment, I can choose to stay in my place of power, not react, and honor my time block.

Or I can allow my phone to dictate my next move.

If I react to the text and respond, you know what's going to happen next.

I'm going to get sucked into a vortex of distraction that will likely end with me scrolling through Instagram Reels and wondering thirty minutes later how the heck I ended up there. And worst of all, I'll have made marginal, if any, progress on the task *I promised myself* I would tackle in that time.

Does this sort of thing ever happen to you? (That wasn't a serious question. Of course it does.)

Next time, remember who's boss. **You.** You are the director of your attention. Decide how you spend your day. Be intentional with the time you've guarded on your calendar. I'm pretty sure you don't have any calendar entries titled, "Play on social media" or "Get sucked into mass family texting," so hold yourself accountable for that time and do what you said you were going to do.

And if you need some assistance, you're in luck. There's this awesome little feature on all phones called "Do Not Disturb," and it is legit. You can even customize it so that your phone will still ring if one of your "Favorite" contacts is trying to call you. I have my kiddos' school saved as a "Favorite," and I feel secure knowing that if some other kid whacks mine in the head with a Badminton racquet, I'll still find out about it even when I'm in Do Not Disturb mode.

No excuses! Turn that sucker on, flip your phone face down, and create before you consume.

Bye–bye, Hot Mess Express! Get out there and crush it.

Chapter Four

··

HANDLING THE MORNING
RUSH LIKE A (MOM) BOSS

What is it about weekday mornings that turns the best of us into total stress balls? On any given Saturday, the sun shines gloriously through kitchen windows everywhere as birds chirp happily and parents and kids alike are properly stuffed with pancakes.

But on a Tuesday? Shoes mysteriously cannot be found, homework folders go missing, and snacks of all kinds forget to make their way into backpacks. (Please tell me this stuff doesn't only happen in my house.) Compound all of those happenings with a kiddo who woke up with an *attitude*, and even the most organized of moms will find themselves begging for mercy.

This irksome phenomenon is one of the sneakiest energy-suckers known to mom-kind, and I have a name for it . . .

The Morning Whirlwind.

The thing that makes the Morning Whirlwind so beastly is that it happens, well, *in the morning*, which means one nasty spin through it can set the tone for your entire day. For me, a rough morning often translates to feeling less powerful, which means that honoring my well-intentioned plans for the day takes serious motivation.

The good news is that the opposite is true—meaning, once you tame the Morning Whirlwind, you can take back your day *and* your power. Double whammy! And it's honestly not all that difficult. If I can do it—*trust me, mama*—you can too. With a few simple tweaks, you can turn that whirlwind into a breeze.

Here's how I play it.

Plan tomorrow's outfit the night before.

If you're going to be heading out the door, getting dressed is something you must think about intentionally.

Nothing robs you of your power faster than not knowing what to wear and wasting precious minutes trying on outfit after outfit when you could be doing something more productive like, I don't know, eating breakfast? Plus, that kind of furious outfit changing often leads to a downward spiral into the land of "I have nothing to wear," which is one stop before, "Nothing looks good on me." Both places should be avoided!

So when I say plan your outfit, I mean plan it to the last detail, including your accessories.

If you have a particularly hectic work week, consider planning your entire week's outfits on Sunday night, before the mayhem of the week begins. This strategy is particularly effective when you first create a rotating uniform of sorts. The "uniform" should consist of several pieces you know look great on you. Old faithfuls, I call them. My "uniform" consists of four dresses I feel great wearing. If I want to get creative and wear something off-uniform, I certainly will. But if I have no idea what to wear, I fall back on the uniform. See how simple?

Planning what to wear the night before is also really effective for your kiddos. Where my children attend school, students are expected to be dressed in compliance with the school's dress code. To avoid any time-consuming, ear-splitting meltdowns, we mos' def' decide on outfits the night before. Easy. Also, not time sucking.

Get a leg up on breakfast before you go to bed.

My kids need to be out the door no later than 7:18 a.m. each morning, which also means they need to be fed before the brushing-teeth-and-getting-socks-and-shoes-on fiasco happens. And since I'll be awake with them, I might as well eat too.

I don't know about you, but for me, scrambling in the kitchen trying to find blender parts or a clean bowl in an effort to serve breakfast whilst ensuring that the small humans in my house are brushing their hair, getting dressed, and heading downstairs *on time* for said meal is like, a major drag. If I haven't figured out the breakfast puzzle ahead of time, more often than not, that story ends with hasty, open-mouthed scarfing of an unsatisfyingly small granola bar and a whole lot of grumbling (mostly from me).

But it doesn't have to be that way.

Why not instead plan breakfast time the way you would plan anything else? The night before, wash the dishes you know you're going to need in the morning so they're ready to go and easy to find. Fill the coffeemaker with water and make sure the filter is clean. Get the coffee beans in the grinder (or measure out the grounds and get them in the filter). I'm a protein shake kind of gal, so I'll compile the ingredients the night before, stick them inside the blending cup and pop the whole thing in the fridge with a lid. If your kids are old enough to help themselves, put bowls and spoons out on the counter and ensure that the milk and cereal are within reach in the fridge and pantry.

Whatever you decide on, just know that the few minutes it takes before bed to get this stuff in order will be well worth it come sunrise. Your mornings will be—if I may be so bold—easy. And don't you love easy?

Slay the hair and makeup beast.

If you are going to be seen by your co-workers, this is where the rubber meets the road.

Unless you're bald and allowed to wear ginormous sunglasses to work, the hair and makeup beast is no joke. Even if you're only attending meetings via video chat, you know as a woman that you have to put forth *some* effort in the looks department, lest people think you're ill or exhausted or—*ouch!*—unprofessional.

In my opinion, there is no greater time sucker in the morning than the hours painstakingly spent on hair and makeup by womankind every day. I've tested a few tricks on myself over the years and have learned how to get ready in half the time it used to take me, and mind you, I have wavy hair that must either be deliberately curled or straightened but cannot be left to its own devices.

Number one on my best-friend list: a wet-to-straight flat iron. It will literally take your hair from wet to dry *and* straight in one step. I find that it works best if your hair has been air drying for about 15 to 20 minutes which, of course, is the perfect time to put on that outfit you already picked out and do your makeup.

Now, a word on makeup.

As a former sales director for one of the largest skincare and cosmetics companies in the world, I know a thing or two about the stuff. And by that, I mean I know the absolute minimum number of products and time you need to look like you made an effort. All it takes is an eyebrow pen (or brow-colored eye shadow and an angled brush), mascara, and tinted lip balm. I prefer lip balm to gloss because it adds just enough color to make you look energized and a mirror isn't needed to apply it, which means you can slather it on quickly, even as you're walking into your destination.

Eyebrows matter the most! If you have time for nothing else, fill in your eyebrows. And definitely wear mascara. At the very least, you'll look like you tried. You'll also look awake, which is generally a good thing.

If I'm not going anywhere, does any of this stuff really matter?

Oh yes, my friend. How you do one thing is how you do everything, and when it comes to having an awesome day, what you create each morning is vital.

Don't forget. Your kiddos are watching everything you do. Show them that the greatest thing they can ever do is love themselves by demonstrating that *you* love *yourself.* Choose to start each day feeling powerful and proud of who you are. Could you go around looking like you just rolled out of bed, pants with zippers be damned? Sure, you *could*. Will you feel powerful? Probably not. And that likely means you won't act powerful either.

Living as your highest and best self means not trading away your beauty and strength, even if you're only going to be seen by folks on Microsoft Teams or at the grocery store. Truly, taking pride in how you were created is a form of self-care. And, as we just established, it doesn't have to take forever or even cause a frenzied mess.

So tomorrow morning, tame that morning whirlwind.

You've totally got this.

Chapter Five

....

DECLUTTER YOUR HOME (AND YOUR LIFE) WITH THIS RIDICULOUSLY EASY TRICK

Have you ever opened a closet or a cupboard and thought, "Yeesh, when did we accumulate all this *stuff*?"

Duh, that's a rhetorical question because you're a mom, and therefore, *of course you have.*

Once during my husband's 13-year tenure with his former employer, he and I were seriously considering an opportunity in his career that would have required us to move out of state. One day during the lengthy interview process, I opened a cabinet under my bathroom sink, saw all the clutter, and thought, "Am I *really* going to pack all of this and move it? And if not, then why am I keeping it—even if we don't move?"

That one question helped me declutter every drawer, cabinet, and closet in my house.

I didn't do it overnight, or even in one week. But once I started, it became my priority every time I had five or ten minutes to spare. I would ask myself that question as I went through all of our stuff—toiletries, Tupperware, toys, clothes, linens, *everything*.

And let me tell you: it was so cathartic. Not only did I purge a bunch of stuff I was no longer using and create a much more organized home, I was able to donate most of the items to charity, which felt really good.

In the end, we didn't end up moving. But it was still a worthwhile exercise because it allowed me to declutter my home, and in turn, my life! Listen to me, mama: do not underestimate how much easier your life can be when your space isn't threatening to suffocate you with one more flipping Lego set.

So, if you have a little or—*ahem*—a lot of clutter in your house, pick one drawer, one cabinet, or one closet and try this hack. Whether you're moving or not, it's quite effective.

Now I know you might be thinking, "But wait! What if I do end up needing this stuff? That's why I'm keeping it! Because I might one day need it again!"

Listen, I hear ya. I often have had that hoarder-like mentality too.

But if you haven't used it in more than a year, the truth is, you're probably not gonna.

And if parting with it still feels too final, just grab one of those big plastic storage bins with a lid from Target and put the stuff that doesn't meet the "would I pack this and move it" test in there. Then, find a place for the bin in your garage. If after another six months to a year, you still haven't touched it, it's time to say goodbye.

Here's to making room in our lives for what matters most.

Chapter Six

THE POWER OF A MORNING ROUTINE

I know, yawn.

Everyone is always talking about creating a morning routine, and waking up early, and *blah blah blah*. One day, I finally decided to see why people are always yapping about it. And that's when I learned the truth.

Morning routines are legit.

As moms, we are always on call. Literally. If my kids are awake, I can guarantee I'll be hearing, "Mom!" at least twenty times throughout the course of a single day. Sometimes they call me to ask for a snack. Other times they need help finding something and believe I have a magical honing device that can conjure lost sweatshirts, face masks, or homework out of thin air. Sometimes they've hurt themselves and need a kiss and a snuggle. Most often, though, it's to tattle on each other.

At this stage of their lives, my kids depend on me for a lot. It's beautiful. And it's exhausting.

That's why "alone time" is the one thing I crave more than anything, and if you're like most moms I know, you crave it too.

The question is, how do we get it?

This is where a morning routine comes in.

I won't claim it's a one-size-fits-all solution, but after a ton of trial and improvement, I do know it works for me.

An intentional morning routine comes with guaranteed "me" time. Now, let me assure you that "morning routine" is not my cute way of telling you to wake up at 5 a.m. But if you're not currently getting time to yourself every single day, I *am* telling you to wake up earlier than you are now.

OK, before you skip this chapter, hear me out!

Waking up earlier doesn't have to be painful. Promise.

You only need 20 minutes to yourself—before everyone else in your house gets up—to "fill your cup," so to speak. What you do in those 20 minutes is entirely up to you. Maybe you sit somewhere cozy and enjoy your first, blissful cup of coffee without anyone interrupting you. You might read that novel you've been meaning to dig into, or meditate, journal, or exercise. I use those first 20 minutes of the day to work on my biggest, hairiest, most audacious goal.

Whatever you do with that time, I strongly urge you to spend it on something you love. Something that's *just for you.*

Now, if you're shaking your head at me like, "Girl, I snooze three times before I make it out of bed as it is. How am I supposed to wake up twenty minutes earlier?!"

I got you, girlfriend.

Here's what I suggest: start by waking up five minutes earlier. Just five. (You've got five in you, come on.)

Once you have that down, set your alarm for 10 minutes earlier. And when you're rocking 10, move it to 15. Eventually, you'll get to 20 minutes like it ain't no thing. The best part is that, as you're working your way there, you're getting an extra five, ten, or fifteen minutes in your day of *guaranteed alone time.* Take a sec' to imagine how glorious that would be.

You're a morning routine away from making it happen.

To really seal the deal, I also suggest going to sleep at the same time every night (and no, that's not code for, "Go to bed at 8 p.m."). My go-to bedtime is 10 p.m., which allows me to honor my body's needs. (Like a koala bear, I love to sleep. If I don't get enough, I'm kind of—totally—a monster.)

To help me stay on track, I use the "Sleep | Wake Up" tool in the alarm section of the built-in clock app on my iPhone. Going to bed at the same time every night solidifies my routine in the morning and allows me to get seven and a half hours of sleep before I'm up at 5:30 a.m. to enjoy the peace, quiet, and productivity that comes with the stillness of my household at that hour. I've worked my way up to a sixty-minute morning routine, which, in addition to allowing me to work on my BHAGs, gives me time to meditate, journal, and pray.

Try it this week.

Decide what you would do with guaranteed alone time. Then set your alarm for five minutes earlier than it is now (or twenty if you're feeling robust) and start going to sleep at the same time every night.

You got this, mama. I'll be thinking of you as I'm sipping on my peppermint tea tomorrow morning.

Chapter Seven

<hr>

STOP TREATING YOURSELF
LIKE GARBAGE

I threw my tennis racquet at my coach once.

OK, in fairness, I didn't throw it at him to hit him. I just threw it forcefully across the net and it went flying in his general direction. Thankfully, it landed at his feet without touching him. And he was very gracious when I apologized. "Did I say something to upset you?" he'd asked.

"No," I'd grumbled. "I'm just frustrated with myself." Or more specifically, with my seeming lack of ability on the tennis court. That day's practice did not get any better and ended with me letting out a scream worthy of a cockroach sighting when I missed yet another easy ball. I recall one of my teammates scolding me disdainfully from the neighboring court.

"DEAL WITH IT!" I'd yelled back at her. But like a crazy lady. I acted like a crazy lady.

Walking off the court, I demanded to know from my coach if I could demote myself and move down to a lower division. "No, Nikki," he'd said patiently, shaking his head. "You're already on the roster for this division. That's against the rules."

I knew that rule full well, of course.

"Then can I get my money back?" I'd snapped.

He looked me in the eye then. "You want to quit?"

I jutted my chin out and crossed my arms. "Maybe. I suck."

I'm laughing at myself as I recall the memory now. (The way I say that, you'd think it happened years ago when I was a teen. It didn't. I was a full-on grown up with two kids and a minivan.) And while objectively one could say I did not display my best behavior, or that I acted like a petulant, adolescent girl, I'm actually proud of my ability to freely release my emotions. It's not the way I behaved that day that bothered me afterward.

What I hated about this experience was the cause of my meltdown in the first place. I'd felt it before, a familiar weight in the middle of my chest that quickly built into tears threatening to spill out of my eyes.

It was that voice repeating itself in my mind, over and over, *"You're not good enough. You don't belong here."*

And it didn't stop there, as evidenced by my assault and near-battery of my coach with my racquet. My stinkin' thinkin' quickly spiraled into, *"Why would another mom ever take advice from you? How could anyone ever be inspired by you?"*

I found myself desperately trying to claw my way back into being positive and graceful, and then viciously berating myself when I wasn't able to do so.

Later, I recounted the story to someone I deeply admire and respect, and she described my tantrum as the equivalent of having one foot on the gas and the other on the brake at the same time.

Yeah, that's a head-smacking, painfully accurate analogy if I've ever heard one.

You know, as gritty, determined, and resilient as I am, my "I suck" moments sure are intense. Despite knowing on some level that I'm pretty awesome, having been fearfully and wonderfully made and all that, sometimes I feel like someone has me handcuffed, blindfolded, and gagged.

And, having witnessed my fellow moms inflict this sort of vitriol on themselves again and again, I know I'm not alone.

I'm naming this culprit the "You-Can't Monster." We all have one. She's an insidious thing, lurking in our minds waiting to pounce on us anytime we think of stepping into our greatness.

You know who I'm talking about. She's always saying you can't afford it, you don't deserve it, you won't be any good at it. She rolled her eyes at you when you considered starting a side hustle and ticked off on her mean little fingers all the reasons you wouldn't succeed. She shook her head when you thought you might sign up to run a 5K and reminded you how hard it would be to train and how *not* athletic you are. And when you decided to put your soul on the internet and start a podcast dedicated to empowering other moms, she raised her eyebrows at you and laughed.

I don't know about your You-Can't Monster, but mine is a real bitch.

So how do we combat her? Well first, we must accept that our respective You-Can't Monsters only exist because we created them. Don't get me wrong—we didn't create them intentionally. It happened slowly, over time, the culmination of not-so-nice experiences dating back to when we were kids. Someone told us the picture we colored wasn't good enough or refused to play Four Square with us. Someone else made fun of our ideas or slid away from us when we tried to sit next to them on the bench at lunch. They told us our dark, curly hair looked stupid or that our outfit was ugly, and before we knew it, a part of us started believing them. And silently, it happened. Your You-Can't Monster was created, and you didn't even know it!

But there's good news. What you create, you can also dis-create. (Is that a word?)

A few years ago, I worked intensely with a self-discovery trainer whose professional life is dedicated to training others how to harness their God-given power. She helped me realize that my You-Can't Monster only rears her head when I'm not *being* who I *am*.

I am kind. I am loved. I am important.

And so are you. You are kind. You are loved. You are important.

As I've reflected on this truth over the years, I've realized that a kind, loved, important person does not tell herself she sucks. And she definitely does not do it repeatedly.

Would you ever—as in, like, *ever*—speak to your child the way you so often speak to yourself? Would you tell your daughter she isn't good enough? Would you tell your son he doesn't matter?

Um, Imma go out on a limb over here and say, "No."

So stop doing it to yourself. Right now. Cold turkey. Listen, I understand that years of self-doubt are not easily erased, and it's not always possible to control your first thought. But your *second* thought? Take responsibility for your second thought. Treat yourself like the kind, loved, important person you are.

Now when my You-Can't Monster shows up (and she does), I know what to do. I'll admit that it still takes me a minute to get her fangs out of my neck, but eventually I remember that I get to decide my second thought. The other day, she popped in at my tennis match and started running her mouth. I responded out loud (under my breath, mind you, so as not to alert my opponents or my partner to the fact that I was *literally* talking to myself), and said, "You can do whatever you want. I'm kind, I'm loved, and I'm important. I decide. I am winning this point."

And I did. After that, my partner and I went on to win many, many points and we won the match emphatically. (In a related story, that post-match glass of Sancerre tastes so much better when you win.)

The next time your You-Can't Monster shows up and starts throwing her annoying weight around to ruin your day, tell her what's up. You are kind. You are loved. You are important.

Ain't nobody got nothin' on you, beautiful.

Chapter Eight

....

UNLEASH YOUR
INNER BADASS

Why do anything—seriously, *anything*—if you aren't going to give yourself the full experience?

Feel into that question. And yes, you read it right. You give to yourself fully or you hold yourself back. No one else is involved, my friend, and that is the #wholetruth.

This concept reminds me of that old cliché, "dance like no one is watching." You've heard it before, surely. Perhaps during a heart-to-heart, you've told someone else to live that way. Heck, you might even have that saying on a placard on your wall somewhere.

It seems we all *understand* what it means to dance like no one is watching. But do we *feel* it?

I'll admit I've most definitely lived most of my life worrying that people are watching, and that they're judging my every move as a wife and a mother. I have an identity who is fiercely attached to following rules. That rule-following part of me enjoys being accurate and correct, and doing things the way they're "supposed" to be done. She enjoys being told, "Yes! You did it right!" No doubt, it was because of that identity I graduated first in my class from law school. Literally *no one* did better than I did that year. Not. A. One. Suffice it to say, I know what it means to execute impeccably.

It's a safe, comfortable place for me to be.

On the flip side of that identity is a gut-wrenching, hysterical fear of making a mistake. What if people are indeed watching me dance? What if I'm not doing it right? What if I fall? What if I screw up and people *see*?

That fear has existed within me my entire life and, despite my success on paper, it has stifled me. For every A+ there is a tantrum I've thrown, the kind where I've ripped to shreds the coloring book pages showing my crayon marks outside the lines. Behind every award there's hair I've ripped from my own head strewn on the floor. For as long as I can remember, getting it right was all that ever mattered.

The result, ironically, is that I didn't turn up the dial and fully use my gifts. Except for a few stand-alone moments, I never played full-out. I didn't allow myself to simply be one with the experience. I have always had an eye on the outcome.

That's why I rip unreturnable tennis balls with graceful, deliberate power in practice but shrink into myself and merely dink balls over the net during a real match. It's why I belt out tunes in my car but only hum at church. It's why I married my ex-husband, who I knew wasn't in love with me. It's why I stayed even after he told me to leave. It's why I went through with a wedding that should never have been.

I never wanted to admit a *mistake*. I couldn't stand the thought of failing.

What I didn't realize until now is that admitting the mistake and walking into the unknown to find real love—even at the risk of failure— still would have allowed me to claim a win. And that's true of every scenario in which I've held myself back. Even if I had been single for awhile; even if balls go flying off my racquet into the fence; even if I sing off key, I can still win at giving myself the full experience. *I can still win* because I'll never wonder what could have been if I had played full-out instead of holding back for fear of doing it wrong.

Allowing yourself to feel it all is the win, girlfriend.

The most hilarious part of this revelation is that when you're playing full-out instead of playing not to lose, you're much more likely *not to lose*.

You're giving yourself the best shot at getting what you wanted (and were so fearful of losing) in the first place.

When I finally surrendered, I was able to give myself an amazing experience at something as innocuous as a graduation party. I let myself be totally immersed in conversations without wondering who else might be there or what I might be missing out on by giving one person at a time my clear, neutral attention. I got up on a stage and danced my heart out, indeed, as if no one was watching. I didn't care at all if I was "doing it right" or if I looked stupid.

As it turns out, someone was watching. My adoring husband. And you know what? I didn't look stupid. I looked confident and happy. He was drawn to me like a magnet. We had more fun than we had in months. We had a *blast*.

I want my children to see me living that way. I want to model for them that they can shine *even if* other people are watching them. I want them to know they can trust themselves by showing *I trust myself.*

Don't you want that for your kids?

Don't you want to show them what it looks like to embrace their God-given gifts and live life *unleashed?* Let's be done with not giving ourselves the full experience. Let's live our lives emphatically, in capital letters.

If you lose while giving it your all, so be it. You'll win at playing full-out, at being all in with the process, at not leaving *anything* on the table or bottled inside.

You are a bold, unapologetic badass. Let that girl out.

Chapter Nine

HOW TO START SOMETHING NEW (EVEN IF IT SCARES THE CRAP OUT OF YOU)

Like the phoenix that bursts into flames, burns to ash, and rises to begin life again, I have started over a lot.

Going down in flames and pulling myself up to start again from ash has taught me the greatest lessons of my life. In my short—*ahem*—42 years, I've left an entire life behind on one continent and started anew on another. I've ended a marriage that wasn't working and stepped into pain and uncertainty to find true love and compatibility on the other side. I've walked away from a lucrative legal career to be a stay-at-home mom, created a kickass home-based business as a direct seller, and then moved on to become a mom coach extraordinaire. I've let go of perfectionism to embrace raw, vulnerable beingness. (That one is an ongoing lesson, I'll be the first to admit.)

People ask me all the time how I'm able to begin again and again and continually see success.

The answer came to me one day when I was kayaking, something I only do once a year. I had stopped paddling so my daughter and I could enjoy the view for a moment. It was a beautiful day in Sanibel, Florida and, despite the light breeze, the water was totally flat, like glass. After a few minutes, she turned back to look at me.

"Can we try to catch up with Daddy and Ryan now, Mommy?"

"Sure," I said, dipping my paddle into the water. The nose of our kayak had slowly drifted off course while we had been still, and I now needed to turn us. But to my surprise, it was like rowing through mud. I couldn't believe how strenuous it was to change directions.

Eventually though, thanks to my super-duper strong shoulder muscles, we got going. Once we were gliding again, turning the kayak was a breeze. And that's when it hit me.

It's much easier to change directions when you're moving than it is from a dead stop.

And that, my friends, is the reason I'm able to see success each time I've started over. Quite simply, it's because I'm willing to dig in and *start moving*. Most of us are so scared of what could happen if we start something new that we remain stationary, paddle poised over the water but never breaking the surface.

The uncertainty is paralyzing.

As time passes, the thought of moving gets scarier and scarier. We worry that we won't be able to go in the direction we want. We fear that we won't know what the second step should be.

But here's the thing, girlfriend: you don't need to know what the second step will be to make the first one.

Once you start, the next step will reveal itself.

If it turns out you take a "wrong" step along the way, just change directions. Likely, the reason you created the experience of the "wrong" step in the first place is so you could reveal to yourself, in no uncertain terms, what you need to shift. And, like my experience in the kayak, because you're already moving, changing directions will be a lot easier than it was to begin.

I know, I know. Time for a You-Can't Monster check, because right now yours is making a nasty face and saying, "Easier said than done!" Well, as my friend Chris Ruden would say, "Done is better than said." As Chris points out, and you have to agree, everything that requires action—literally *everything*—is easier said than done. Is it easier to say you're going to wash your hair than it is to actually wash it? Yep. Just like it was easier to say I wanted to be in a healthy, loving relationship than it was to pack my things, move out, and file for divorce.

So, since we're strong mamas setting examples for our kids, let's stop using that phrase as a crutch. Just because it's easier to say something than it is to do it doesn't mean it can't be done.

And guess what? It probably will be hard at first, like my first drags of the paddle through the water that day. Starting over has been exactly like that for me—every time, it's hard. But I keep going. And every time, the next step reveals itself.

Now, here's where stuff gets real.

The reason I write stuff like this is because I need a little smack on the tush. I myself want to start new things—constantly—and I am always absolutely terrified about taking the first step.

TERRIFIED.

I'm afraid I won't know what I'm doing. I'm afraid no one will like it. I'm afraid I won't do a good job. You know, the usual.

In an effort to get myself going, I gather research and data. In other words, I actually *know* most of the time what the first few steps are! And yet sometimes, I find myself sitting here, stationary, months later.

So trust me, you're not alone if you feel like you've been standing at the precipice for awhile, wanting to jump into your dream yet holding yourself back in sheer terror of what will happen next. But what you and I both need to remember is that great things never came from comfort zones. The magic happens out *there*, beyond the precipice.

In *You are a Badass*, Jen Sincero says, "You are the only you there is and ever will be. Do not deny the world its one and only chance to bask in your brilliance." Words to live by, don't you think? Truly, where would we all be if our heroes who came before us never took that first step? You and I might not even have a smartphone on which to post on social media about how stuck we are!

Wherever you're holding yourself back, *just start.*

Drag your paddle through that water. You cannot forget, even when it's terrifying and hard, that you are destined for greatness.

Because you know what? You can do terrifying, hard things. (And yes, I'm talking to myself, too.)

Chapter Ten

YOUR PERFECTIONISM IS SUCKING THE JOY OUT OF MOTHERHOOD

In case you haven't noticed, motherhood and perfectionism do not make a winning combination. And I've tried to combine them. Believe me, I've tried.

Merriam Webster defines "perfectionist" as ~~Nikki Oden~~ "an individual who exhibits or adheres to perfectionism," which, in turn, is defined as "a disposition to regard anything short of perfection as unacceptable."

For me, it goes much deeper than that.

A perfectionist ties her identity and her worth to her performance.

For as long as I can remember, I've put intense pressure on myself to perform. As you might imagine, that kind of pressure has an ugly side. My perfectionism has often gone hand-in-hand with a *ton* of negative self-talk. Historically, I have been brutally hard on myself. When people would point out to me how mean I could be to myself, I would often reply (snidely, with a sourpuss face), "No one ever got anywhere in life by being easy on themselves."

I can be a major pill, I know.

Being a perfectionist is not entirely bad, though. (Do I sound defensive?) Certainly you'd want a perfectionist as your kid's neurosurgeon or the calligrapher for your sister's baby shower invitations, yes? There is value in taking your work seriously and wanting to produce the absolute best results. Without a doubt, my perfectionism led to me graduating first in my class from law school and managing Type 1 Diabetes for two full-term pregnancies without any complications.

When harnessed deliberately and used in proper doses, perfectionism can yield unparalleled results.

But when I became a mother, I walked face-first into the realization that those folks who told me to be easier on myself were right. Being a perfectionist has kept me from appreciating my mistakes, which have taught me my greatest life lessons. It has robbed me of enjoying small wins.

And I do *not* want to model that type of behavior for my children.

Plus, do you think perfection is even in the realm of possibility when you have a one-week-old, or when you're sleep training, or when you're teaching your kid how to pee in a toilet?

Ba ha ha ha!

I quickly realized I was going to be in for a whole lot of heartache and miss out on a whole lot of joy if I didn't lose my death grip on achieving "perfection."

Here's what helped me.

Be here, now.

Stop listening to the chatter inside your brain.

You know what I mean—the voice playing out in minute detail what "might" happen or what "could" go wrong, or that wants to remind you of all those times in your past when things didn't go as smoothly as you had hoped.

None of that is real. It either already happened or might never, ever happen. The only thing that exists is this moment, right now. Get out of your head and experience it.

It's really nice out here.

Flip the script.

Instead of asking yourself, "What if I fail?" or "What if they criticize me?" Ask yourself, "How can I create something *worth* criticizing?"

Perfectionists tend to be rule-followers. We are fiercely attached to doing things correctly because we are terrified of getting it "wrong." That fear can be paralyzing. As a coping mechanism, many perfectionists convince themselves it would be better not to try than to try, and subsequently fail or be criticized.

But would you ever be OK with your kids not even trying just because they're scared they might "fail?"

Heck no.

You'd flip the script for them and explain that trying is the only way to learn and get better. So why aren't you doing that for yourself?

As an entrepreneur who creates content for a living, I now always ask myself this question before pressing "publish" or "send:" *Did I create something worth criticizing?* If I'm not creating something that's even worth criticizing, I have bigger problems than whether the end product is perfect. But more importantly, flipping the script on myself gets me out of paralysis and into *action.*

Flip the script and get out there. Run for the PTA board. Ask for the promotion. Write the book. Who knows? It just might work out.

Just start.

For real. Just start. Unless we're talking about imminent bodily harm or threats to human life, there is no point in worrying about what could or might go wrong.

You don't need to know what the second step will be to take the first one. Use the information you have right now, and just take one step. The next step will always reveal itself. Rest in knowing there are no bad outcomes.

If you discover you took a "wrong" step along the way, course-correct with the next step. It's much easier to switch directions when you're moving than it is from a dead stop, anyway.

Change your vocabulary.

As a perfectionist, you probably hate the word "mistake." So, change your vocabulary.

Instead of viewing mistakes as "screw-ups" or "messes" or other undesirable results, allow yourself to see them for what they actually are: teachers. Mistakes are our greatest teachers, if we'll allow them to be. The truth is that we only grow by making mistakes.

I married the wrong guy once. I was so concerned with checking boxes and ticking off what I thought should come next on my list of life's achievements that I didn't bother to stop and think about whether we were compatible (we weren't). After five years of being together, we were married for eight measly months before I filed for divorce. I almost stayed, because I was so terrified of being viewed as a failure. I almost allowed that fear to paralyze me into perpetuating years of what would have been a miserable union.

But because I didn't give in to the fear, I met the love of my life.

Fifteen years, two kids, and one hellacious pandemic later, we're still totally into each other. That one decision—to step out of my comfort zone, own the mistake, and choose to learn from it—has allowed me to experience joy and love like I might not ever have otherwise known.

Next time you're faced with stepping outside of your comfort zone and getting out there, instead of saying, "I hope I don't make a mistake," ask yourself, "I wonder what I'll discover?"

Figure out what not to do.

When it comes to growing and scaling my business, I almost never get it right on the first try. In other words, I put myself out there and experience a lot of things a perfectionist might argue are avoidable if I had just waited until everything was "perfect."

But I view those errors as a guide for what *not* to do on the next try. Figuring out quickly what doesn't work saves me a ton of time and heartache. If something I create isn't going to obtain the results I ultimately want, I'd rather know that sooner than later. Wouldn't you?

The same applies to any new endeavor, even the less scary ones, like trying a new dinner recipe. Yes, it can be frustrating to stumble as you're starting something new (or when you cook something for the first time and everyone at the table has a comment about it), but there is tremendous value in discovering what doesn't work.

Allowing yourself to become paralyzed by perfectionism will certainly keep you safe in your comfort zone, but you're missing out on vital information you could be collecting on how to improve by getting out there and making so-called "mistakes."

Feedback is a gift. Go get yours.

Most of all, remember to be nice to yourself. When you hold yourself to an impossible standard, you probably won't give yourself much grace. But hear me, mama. Not every meal is going to be homemade. The mail won't always be sorted. You will be late when your kiddos can't find their shoes.

Did you feed your children today, though? Do they have beds to sleep in and clothes to wear? Do they feel safe and loved?

Then it's OK. Motherhood is just as messy as it is beautiful. It will never be perfect.

Because by the way, "perfect" doesn't exist.

Chapter Eleven

....

YOU AIN'T NO QUITTER

Did you know there's a day named after people who quit their goals?

I'm serious. It's called "Quitter's Day," and it takes place every year on January 19th. The term was coined in 2019 by fitness platform Strava after conducting a study involving 800 million people (no, but literally, 800 *million* people) in which they discovered that January 19th is the day 80% of folks give up on the goals they set in the New Year.

Dang! So soon!

I'll admit that I was shocked to learn this statistic. I thought most people *at least* made it to the first week in February, but after giving it some thought, I suppose it's not all that surprising.

After all, when we close out one year and head into the next, we're excited. We're idealistic.

And sometimes, we're also unrealistic.

Now, let's get one thing straight. I hate the word "realistic" when it comes to goal setting. Despite what conventional goal-setting wisdom might tell you, setting huge goals is the way to go. I'm in the "set-crazy-un-realistic-ginormous" goals camp.

But realize there's a difference between setting a goal so big it terrifies you, and taking a first step toward that goal that's just as big.

Remember, although your goals every year should be audacious and should, in fact, be borderline unrealistic, it's OK—in fact, it's necessary—to start small. Oftentimes when we give up on a big goal quickly, it's only because the first step we attempted to take in achieving it was way too big.

If that's you, trust me, you're not alone. Here's how you get back on track (and a quick review of Chapter Three).

First, start with what you're going to have to accomplish on a monthly basis. What action step can you take each month that, if done consistently for 12 months, would result in you achieving your big, hairy, audacious goal? Notice I said step, as in one. Singular. You're simply deciding on one monthly milestone. So, for example, if your big goal was to lose 100 pounds, your monthly milestone might be to lose 8 pounds.

But if you're going to stay focused (and away from the quitter's table), we've gotta trim it down even more.

Next, decide on the one activity you can do this week to ensure you achieve your monthly milestone.

Often as you're puzzling over this question, your first several responses will be milestones as well. Keep asking yourself the question until you get down to an activity. Using the weight-loss example, the activity might be to walk five miles. (Side note: Remember you're coming up with something you *can* do. There's no point in choosing something that sounds juicy and impressive, but you know you won't actually do because it's too hard or time consuming.)

Finally, shrink it down to the itty bitty by asking yourself, "What's the one task I can do each day to ensure I complete my weekly activity?" Go as small as you can until you get down to a single task. In keeping with the weight-loss example, perhaps the task might be something as simple as, "Be in bed with face washed and teeth brushed by 9:30 p.m.," because that will guarantee you wake up on time to go for your walk.

Did you see what we did there? We took something big, hairy, and audacious and made it bite-sized.

You ain't no quitter, mama! Get back on that horse. Or that workout plan. Or . . . you know what I'm saying.

Chapter Twelve

....

STOP SAYING YES
ALL THE TIME

Breaking up with someone is never easy.

And I'm not even talking about a *real* breakup, where you have to re-claim your toothbrush or empty some drawer space and you might actually cry. I'm talking about those awkward "I'd-rather-be-getting-a-pap-smear" moments when you have to turn someone down. Saying "no" can be down-right uncomfortable, so what do we find ourselves repeatedly doing instead?

Not saying anything at all. Or worse, saying yes and then feeling very pissed off.

Now, I can only speak for myself, but I'd be willing to bet good money that when you're the one doing the asking, you would much rather receive an honest "no" than a resentful "yes." And I'm certain you wouldn't want someone to pretend to be interested when they're not, or completely ignore you. So why do we operate this way ourselves?

One reason: in general, women *hate* to say no.

As women, we so often want to keep the peace. We want to please others and try to make them happy. I believe it's simply the way God made us. When harnessed deliberately, this behavior serves us well in our relationships. But when we aim to please others at our own expense, we give away our power. And that, my friend, is *no bueno.*

We've all been there, though.

Surely you remember that time your neighbor roped you into participating in her cookie exchange (which you later found out required five dozen baked-from-scratch cookies that couldn't be the same flavor as anyone else's cookies and oh, can you make them gluten free?). Or that time your kid's preschool asked if you could, pretty please, call every single parent who signed up to bring an item for the upcoming classroom party to remind them of exactly what they had signed up to bring and, despite the fact that these people are grownups who can read and presumably have the bandwidth to remember a bag of chips, you graciously agreed through gritted teeth.

Saying yes when you want to say no is a guarantee for stress and pull-your-hair-out resentment.

So here's what we must remember when we're faced with having to say no: if we do, no one is going to die. If you choose not to be the secretary of the school advisory council, or head of the PTA holiday fundraiser, or serve on the board of directors for your favorite charity, I promise you, no one will *actually* die.

Years ago, I learned this lesson when I was faced with having to turn down a proposal from a woman whose services I was considering for my business. I ultimately decided to go in another direction but the thought of telling her no was *killing* me. It didn't help that I liked her personally and believed she was totally capable of getting the job done. Saying yes, however, simply didn't feel right.

So, what did I do? I played ostrich for a couple of weeks and intentionally stuck my head in the sand, pretending that if I ignored the issue long enough it would forget about me and go away. I hemmed and hawed and made up a bunch of stories in my head about how I didn't want to hurt her feelings and that she'd take the hint from my silence, *et cetera, et cetera, et cetera.*

That got old fast, though. I started thinking about what I would want if I was the one waiting to hear back. And I knew what I had to do.

I picked up the phone, old school, and called her. I didn't hide behind a text or an email. I told her the honest truth, and you know what? She was very gracious and professional about it. Oh, and bonus: neither of us died.

That evening, I got an email from her *thanking* me. She said every now and then she'll prepare a proposal for a potential client and not hear back and she always wonders why. She actually appreciated that I told her no and didn't leave her hanging.

Will wonders never cease! You see? Be the change you want to see in the world! Teach your children how to live in alignment with their values by actually living that way yourself. That kind of unapologetic confidence is born from being decisive.

And decisiveness swings both ways. It *is* OK to say yes. Just make sure when you give a yes, it's your *best* yes—one that aligns with what you want your life to look like. Only commit your time if you'll be making the best use of your gifts or you're getting out of your comfort zone to become a better version of yourself.

For example, although I feel a twinge of sympathy when the PTA fundraising coordinator at my children's elementary school begs via email for volunteers to help her painstakingly sort and bag BoxTops to redeem at ten cents a pop to raise money, sorting through BoxTops is not my best yes. That's why I say no.

And here's the kicker: by saying no, I make room for someone else to give *her* best yes.

Take my neighbor and dear friend, Lara. She's a BoxTop-sorting *ninja*. She can also throw a party that would rival anything (and I do mean *anything*) you could ever find on Food Network or HGTV combined, and she can actually enjoy herself as hordes of people traipse through her house, probably spilling wine and definitely dropping crumbs everywhere as they nosh on delicious morsels from the menu she created.

Clearly, she and I have different strengths. By saying yes to our strengths and no to everything else, we each add value to the world in distinct but necessary ways. And more importantly, instead of being mediocre at everything and making a merely neutral impact, we are laser-focused on our wheel houses and make impacts that are powerful and positive.

Remember that time invested in one area is time away from another. If it's not your best yes, *don't say yes.* Give someone else the opportunity to shine and give *her* best yes. See how beautifully that works out?

Next time you're faced with having to say no to something that's not in alignment with your best life, say it. You can still be your warm and fuzzy self. Just be powerful enough to reply, "If I say yes to this, then I'd be saying no to [myself] or [time with my family] or [time I blocked to work out] or [(fill in the blank)]."

And if saying it on the spot feels too scary, you can always fall back on, "Let me give it some thought and I'll get back to you." Give yourself some time to think, pray, or feel about it, come up with kind but honest words to use, and then get back to that person and just say no.

Chapter Thirteen

IF YOU WANNA HAVE IT ALL, YOU ABSOLUTELY CANNOT DO IT ALL

One of the most valuable lessons I ever learned about success and womanhood came to me at a breakfast event I attended when I was just a young whipper snapper toiling away for Big Law.

The keynote speaker was a global department head for one of the most powerful banks on the planet. Although her success on paper was objectively quite impressive, it seemed to magnify when she revealed she was also a wife and a mother of two. You could practically hear the women in the crowded audience thinking, "*Damn*, girl!"

After a mostly forgettable speech, she took a question from the audience. The inquirer, who seemed quite pleased with herself for coming up with something original to ask, said into the microphone, "How do you achieve balance?"

The speaker literally snorted, and I perked up immediately.

"*Balance?*" she repeated, almost choking on her laughter. "I don't have balance!" She cackled as if the question was meant to be a joke. Realizing it wasn't, she elaborated. "I mean, I love my husband and my kids, but I don't have time to cook them dinner every night." It seemed as if it was all she could do not to wave her hand dismissively. "Ladies, you do not achieve this level of success in business by having 'balance.' I focus on what's most important and pay someone else to take care of the rest."

At that point, I think I actually did say it out loud. "*Damn*, girl!"

I was so impressed, I almost whistled, and not because I want to be the head of some global conglomerate (yet, anyway!). In fact, the business acumen of this woman is the least relevant part of the story. What struck me was her unapologetic honesty in conceding what it *really* takes for her to be great at what she does. I took away this lesson, and it has stayed with me ever since:

There are literally hundreds of things that must be done in your life each day, but they do not all need to be done by *you*.

When you're a mom, it's easy to forget that truth. On a daily basis, we tend to put our own needs last, reacting first to what's urgent (though not necessarily important), and getting mired down in everything that needs to be done without regard to whether we need to be the one doing it.

And when we allow that to happen, we also forget we were made for greatness. We forget that God gave us gifts and told us to shine.

Even on the days when you remember that you were born to make an impact on this world, the question remains: how do you actually *do* that without getting distracted by the gazillion little things all mothers are tasked with from the moment we open our eyes each morning?

The answer is outsourcing.

Truly, you and I do have the same twenty-four hours each day as Beyoncé. The difference with what we do in those hours is how much we're able to outsource. To do great things, you must allow someone else to perform the tasks on your list you don't absolutely love doing or aren't contributing to your life's purpose.

And let's be clear: your life's purpose includes making romantic, alone time for you and your spouse and playing with your kids. It also most definitely includes taking care of *yourself*, to nurture the one and only body God gave you, to meditate, journal, or pray, to indulge in a mani/pedi, and to do whatever else makes you feel warm and happy—even if it's one of the items on my outsourcing list below. Doing things we love is a form of self-care, and self-care is always time well spent.

As a married mother of two and a woman on a mission to change the world one heart at a time through my work, I never have an empty plate. That choice forces me to remember that outsourcing is my friend. It's OK (in fact, when you're a mother, it's necessary) to ask for help. I now understand that I don't need to personally perform every task on my to-do list each week. I need only do what will support me in creating and living out my purpose in life.

Plus, living this way helps to maintain sanity, which is generally a good thing.

These are the ways I invite you to outsource to make your mom life easier.

Stop doing your own grocery shopping and Target runs.

Unless you absolutely love performing these tasks (which would put them in the "self-care" category), you must outsource them. Although they definitely need to be done and sometimes urgently, you and I both know they aren't contributing to your life's purpose.

The solution? Grocery delivery services, like Instacart and Shipt. (Cue the angels singing!) Shipt is pure genius, and you can use it to shop at your favorite stores, like Bed, Bath & Beyond, CVS, Sephora, and Target. You can't buy alcohol using this service, but you can buy almost everything else, from makeup and towels to toothpaste and shampoo to perishable goods, granola bars, and boxed mac 'n cheese.

Here's the best part: it keeps you out of the store itself. Don't get me wrong—I flipping love Target, but every time I set foot in there, I end up spending fifty dollars more than I intended to. Every. Single. Time. By using a service like Shipt instead, I remove all temptation.

It's glorious.

What began as a convenience during the height of the pandemic lockdown has become a new way of life for me when it comes to grocery shopping. I now rely almost exclusively on grocery delivery services, and it has given me back days of my year. If you want to save a little on the fee, do curbside pickup. Yes, it still requires you to drive to the store, but it allows you to skip the up-and-down aisle roaming (and unnecessary spending).

There certainly is a premium for shopping this way, but let's think about what you get in return: your time! Sure, I would spend less if I was clipping coupons and shopping myself—and believe me, I spent years doing that—but the money I saved was negligible compared to the return I'm getting now by using that time to crush my goals and spend quality time with the people I love most.

Same goes for you. Remember, to have it all, you cannot possibly do it all. There are people out there—like your neighborhood delivery service shoppers—who are eager to help you. Let them.

Immediately cease and desist from cleaning your house, doing your laundry, and washing your dishes.

Unless, of course, you absolutely love doing that stuff (and if you do, I really, *really* want to meet you).

If you don't, stop. These tasks are so easily outsourced. Plus, if your family is anything like mine, they won't give a hoot who folded their socks and hung up their shirts. They'll just be happy to have clean clothes at the ready. Same goes for the spotless toilet and crumb-free floor.

My dishwashing, laundry-doing ninja comes once a week. I strategically ask her to come on Mondays so I can start my week off in peace. My house is cleaned every other week, which leaves me with only some touching up to do here and there between cleanings, which I encourage (force) my kids to participate in as a way to teach them responsibility. Does everything get done perfectly? Nope. But done is better than perfect. I transfer that money each week with pleasure.

It's just as honorable to *employ* as it is to *be employed.*

Hiring someone to help you around the house gives that person the opportunity to earn a living and fund their life's purpose, while freeing you up to live yours. See how that works so beautifully?

Don't you dare wash your own car!

I never, ever wash my own car because I don't love doing it. I don't even love driving to a car-washing place to get it done.

But as a mother of two littles, you better believe that my car gets *filthy*. My solution is a mobile car detailing app. The one I use is called Washé. It's like Uber for mobile car detailers. I open the app and select the type of wash I want, and then *voila!* A car detailer in the area will take the job and head to my location. And while my "Washér" is in my driveway washing, waxing, and vacuuming cheddar bunnies from my vehicle, I sit in my house being productive in the air conditioning. When my car has been restored to her shiny, litter-free self, I get a ping and pay the detailer through the app, hands free.

Best. Thing. Ever.

If you don't have a mobile car detailing app that works in your area, ask around for a trusted mobile car detailer. I'm telling you, it's life changing. It's like doing two things at once, only you're doing the thing you want to do and the car detailer is washing your car. Magic!

Oh wait, no, that's just outsourcing.

Let someone else cook dinner for you.

On the two days each week that I leave the house to be a lawyer, I am way too beat when we walk back through the door to cook anything, let alone a meal that resembles wholesome and healthy food. So naturally, I outsource this task instead.

Allowing someone else to cook dinner for me and the three other humans I love most in the world is one of the most powerful ways I take back my time.

My solution is a local chef who prepares meals from a weekly menu he creates. He even has a kids' menu! I peruse online and order what we need for the week, and it appears on my doorstep on Sunday, cooked and ready to be reheated when my family and I are ready to eat. It's absolutely divine. There have been evenings when I've whispered out loud as I'm setting the table, "This totally saved me tonight."

If a hired chef just isn't in your budget, consider using tools you might already have stuffed in a kitchen cupboard somewhere, like a pressure or slow cooker. A slow cooker is an absolute lifesaver. And when it comes to slow cooker meals, Google and Pinterest got your back, girlfriend. There is no shortage of recipes you can lean on that don't require you to chop, dice, or sauté.

You see? You can enjoy a wholesome meal with your family and *you* don't have to cook it!

Oh yes, you can too afford it!

Listen, I understand that all of these outsourcing methods cost money. And no, I don't have piles of it laying around.

So trust me, I get it if your You-Can't Monster is getting all snarky with you right now, glaring at you over her glasses and spewing some nonsense about you not being able to afford to pay someone else to do your chores and run your errands.

But let's get real.

Time invested in one area is time away from another.

And yeah, maybe it means fewer (or zero) runs through the Starbucks drive-thru for a five-dollar-latte, but freeing yourself up to do meaningful work and fund your ideal life simply makes sense.

Maybe that means you can take on more classes as a substitute teacher, or if you're a lawyer like me, performing more legal work you bill for by the hour. Perhaps it means you can accommodate more orders for your custom cookies and cakes. Whatever the payoff, remember that *every time* you choose to use your gifts instead of *wasting* time doing things others can do for you, you're creating your ideal mom life.

And if you're adamant there's not a dime left in your budget to hire someone to help you, start giving some serious thought to who in your life might want to do it for free simply because they love you, like your mom, or your mother-in-law, or your dad's "crazy" aunt.

Now, I'll openly admit that despite my intellectual command of this topic, by no means do I have it all together. I still get mired down in tasks that are urgent but not important. I still find myself wasting precious moments doing things that don't support my best life, like schlepping to the grocery store and refolding towels. The reason I wax poetic about this topic is because I need to be reminded too.

But when I get sucked into the details, I remember a quote from Jamie Gilbert that I've written on my bathroom mirror. "Greatness isn't for the chosen few. Greatness is for the few who choose."

Choose greatness, girlfriend. And start outsourcing.

Chapter Fourteen

MAKE YOURSELF
A "TO-DON'T" LIST

I pride myself on being really good at creating to-do lists. I would go so far as to say I'm a master, if I may be so bold.

The quarantine of 2020, however, was enlightening, to say the least. Thanks to the cancellation of nearly all in-person activities, my plate went from crowded and piled high to having room for another entree. As time passed and more and more events went virtual or were canceled altogether, I started experiencing something profound.

Margin.

Extra time to sleep. Hours to journal daily and read for pleasure. Time to go on morning walks and afternoon bike rides with my kiddos and hubby. Time to write and to cook. To meditate. To intentionally pray.

Once the business of life slowly began to resume, opportunities to add things back to my plate predictably presented themselves, which got me thinking . . . what a perfect time to create a list of things to *stop* doing—or as I like to call it, a "to-don't" list.

I won't claim there's a right or a wrong way to make one, but I will suggest you ask yourself the following focusing questions as you're evaluating what to keep on (and what to scrape off) your plate.

Is this activity serving me?

Put another way, would my life be less rich or joyful without it?

It might seem obvious, but continuing to do something that doesn't serve you is like flooring the gas pedal while slamming on the brake. It's not getting you anywhere. If at worst, an activity is sucking the life out of you, or at best, is simply not adding to your life, stop doing it!

Or you can think about it this way: if you ever found yourself wishing, during the pandemic that this activity might go virtual or be straight-up canceled, it probably (definitely) belongs on your to-don't list. Even certain networking or accountability groups might rightfully find themselves on your to-don't list. Be ruthless as you evaluate whether the activity is adding to your life.

If, on the flip side, you truly would miss the activity, congrats on having discovered, in no uncertain terms, that it should remain in your life!

I feel this way about tennis. During the height of quarantine, my tennis club decided not to participate in the local league. That meant no practices, no matches, and no lessons. And while that also meant I was saving time (and money), I missed it. A lot. I couldn't wait until I could add it back onto my plate.

One thing I stopped missing was working out at a gym. I discovered that my sweat-from-home routine is very challenging—not to mention one I can begin immediately after I roll out of bed and that allows me to step into the shower mere seconds after it's over.

If you're being totally honest with yourself, what's one activity you continue to engage in that isn't serving you? Write that baby on your to-don't list.

Have I formed a healthy new habit that should take priority over the activity I might ditch?

It's easy to focus on what went wrong during the pandemic, and I don't say that flippantly. I know many people lost jobs and even loved ones.

Isn't it also true, though, that some healthy habits took root in our lives?

For me, one such habit is journaling. Although I *love* to write and have kept a diary since I was 11, when I became a mom, journaling fell off my radar. I would buy beautiful journal after beautiful journal and then shove them in my bedside drawer and write them off (pun intended) as something I couldn't make a priority now, but would . . . one day.

Well, "one day" came sooner than I thought. In the early days of quarantine, I found myself with serious writer's block. I started to feel really bummed about it, until my husband suggested I start journaling to get my creative juices flowing again. (Seriously, I love that guy.) So I did, and I fell completely in love with it. It's cathartic and cleansing, and I don't see myself ever stopping.

What about you? Have you recently picked up a healthy new habit? If so, what might have to fall off of your plate to make room for it permanently?

What could I say yes to if I said no to this?

More accurately, what would I have to say no to if I said yes to this?

My friend shared with me that she used to waste tons of time watching mindless television and scrolling through her newsfeed on social media. Remembering that our kiddos are always watching us, she challenged herself to experience her own life instead of someone else's on TV or Instagram. By saying no to those activities, she's been able to say yes to more abundance in her family and professional life.

Remember, time invested in one area is time away from another. As moms, we have a duty to command our time so we can be our highest and best—not only for the people who love and depend on us but for ourselves. When you think of it that way, answering this focusing question becomes a lot easier. The trick is to only give your best yes (and to say no without being mean).

A word of encouragement

Don't freak out!

Just like a to-do list, a "to-don't" or "stop doing" list is fluid. Editable. *Not written in stone.* You can always add to it or remove things from it.

The important thing is that you have a to-don't list, so you can peri-
odically evaluate where you might be giving too much *of* yourself and not
enough *to* yourself.

THE FIVE PEOPLE YOU
HANG AROUND THE MOST

Did you know you are the average of the five people you hang around the most?

It's a potent truth.

It means you essentially share the behaviors and beliefs of the five people you spend the most time with. That's great news if you hang around five people who live intentionally and are generous, confident, and kind. If, on the other hand, you spend most of your time with people who believe their lives are happening to them, complain, are lazy, and settle for mediocrity then, well . . . you know.

You will too.

Acknowledging how much your "Five" influence you is one of the most powerful things you can do. Think about any goal you've been trying to achieve. Depending on the quality of your Five, achieving that goal might be much more difficult than it could be, your great intentions notwithstanding.

Let's take losing weight as an example. If you want to drop a dress size and get healthier, but you're spending most of your time with people who think Doritos and beer are the foundation of a balanced meal or who be-lieve running late counts as exercise, it's exponentially less likely that you'll achieve your goal. Makes sense, right?

But what if your Five consisted of like-minded women who choose health and movement, who cheer you on and call you out and welcome you to do the same for them? Do you think your results would be better?

No doubt, girlfriend.

I'm proud to say that my Five includes three very special women who started as business accountability partners and are now my very best friends. I call these women my Celebration Circle, and I am utterly convinced every mom needs one.

I met Katie, Steph, and Amy when we were all Team Leaders with a now defunct direct sales company. Steph lives in Montana and Katie and Amy are in Wisconsin, so at first we only ever got together at company meetings. Our friendship began with regular check-ins by phone during which we would share business goals and hold each other accountable for completing the commitments we had made on the call before.

Eventually we started communicating more regularly using recorded audio messages on Facebook Messenger. It wasn't long before we began turning to each other for more than just business ideas and accountability. We started to lean on each other, confide in each other, and support each other as mothers, wives, and friends.

Today, I talk to Katie, Steph, and Amy every single day, thanks to an awesome walkie-talkie app we've all downloaded on our phones. I share everything with them, from mom fails to arguments with my husband to things you can only ever talk about with girlfriends. I tell them my biggest dreams and my deepest fears. And because empowered women empower women, they encourage me to be my highest and best.

They challenge me. They give me ideas. They listen to me. They take my side. They openly disagree with me. They defend me. They call me out. They love me fiercely.

They celebrate me. And I do the same for each of them.

Having my Celebration Circle is a huge part of the fullness of my life. But here's the unexpected benefit: having them is also part of my success.

Experiencing the profound effect of a friendship like this makes me want it for everyone, including you. If you don't have a group of women who celebrate and comfort you, who lift you up when you're down and push you to be your best, you need one.

The big question, of course, is how do you create your own Celebration Circle?

This is where the rubber meets the road. Your Celebration Circle will come together as a result of upgrading your Five.

And I'll be the first to tell you that the process will probably be uncomfortable. It requires you to take a long, hard look at some of your existing relationships. But that's the point.

Living your ideal life means surrounding yourself with people whose energy is serving you and the person you want to be.

Here's a great exercise for examining the quality of your Five. Grab a paper and pen and write down the five people you currently hang around the most. Go on. I'll wait.

Once you have your list, write a plus sign (+) next to the people who are adding to the fullness of your life. These are the people who embody what you want more of in your space. Perhaps that's excellence, boldness, intentionality, confidence, positivity, or accountability. Maybe it's mindfulness or creativity or just plain love. There are no wrong answers here. If they're adding to your life, they get a plus sign.

Next, write a zero (0) next to the people who are not necessarily adding to your life, but aren't taking away from it either. These people are Switzerland—they're neutral.

Finally, write a minus sign (-) next to the people who are taking away from the fullness of your life. These are the people who behave like crabs in a bucket. If you've never witnessed this phenomenon, suffice it to say crabs don't hoist each other up when they're trapped in a bucket. It's quite the opposite, in fact. If one of them tries to get out, the others will pull her back down. Literally. Relentlessly. They will keep her from attaining what they perceive as unattainable for themselves.

I've seen human women behave this way as well. Poisoned by a scarcity mindset, they believe if they help another woman succeed there won't be enough success left in the universe for them. And so they pull others down, secretly hoping those women will fail so they can feel better about not excelling. These are the people who drain your energy. They complain, nitpick or nag, and, though you may love them, they make your space toxic.

Now, once you've been raw and honest and identified each person as a positive, a negative, or a neutral, take a look at what you've uncovered. If you don't see five plus signs, you've got some work to do if you want to create a true Celebration Circle. (And duh, of course you want that.)

Although it may seem harsh, that means eliminating the bucket crabs from your Five.

Before you freak out, I'm not suggesting you eliminate them from your *life* (although with certain people, like my ex-husband, that will indeed be the case). You're just removing them from your inner circle. And yes, that's true even if a bucket crab in your Five is someone you're related to, which can make this endeavor extra sticky.

There is no cookie-cutter solution here, and I won't pretend I have one. We're all navigating different dynamics with our relationships. But I do know this: as with any goal, although you're *thinking* big your *actions* must be small.

So instead of completely axing someone from your Five cold turkey, maybe start with something as simple as not engaging when she calls to do her usual unloading of complaints and negativity. Instead of trying to fix things or making suggestions and then getting frustrated when she fights you on them, just let her empty her cup while you listen and remain neutral. Meet her where she is without getting sucked in and let go of expecting her to give you something she can't, like encouragement and support. Turn instead to one of your "plus signs" for those things.

See what I mean? These shifts are small and doable, but they can be total game-changers.

And once your Five consists entirely of plus signs, creating a Celebration Circle is easy.

I don't think there's any right or wrong way to do it, although it's worth noting that my Celebration Circle is completely balanced. If we're talking in terms of MarketForce Styles Indicators, I am the Control, Katie is the Influence, Amy is the Power, and Steph is the Authority. Or if we were witches, I think Amy would be Wind, Steph would be Earth, Katie would be Water, and I would be Fire. Whatever—the point is, we form a balanced circle, which means we each bring different perspectives to goal crushing and problem solving (as well as choosing restaurants, shoes, and wine).

Having a Celebration Circle is fun. Having a quality Five is essential. Having both is a blessing. Choose both, girlfriend. It will change your life.

Chapter Sixteen

PRIORITIZE YOUR SPOUSE
OVER YOUR KIDS

Whenever I say that, there's always one mom who looks at me like I'm wearing my underwear on my face.

If that was you just now, hear me out. Loving your mom life has a whole lot to do with where your marriage falls on your priority list.

My husband, Shawn, and I believe in romance. We spend intentional quality time alone together every week, and we take at least one vacation every year without our kids.

And no, we're not newlyweds!

Maybe it's because we've both been divorced and know what can happen when a relationship falls apart, but without a doubt, focusing on our marriage is the top priority for us. Fifteen years and two kids later, we're still totally into each other.

I've come to understand that romance, date nights, and trips for two are a huge part of loving your life as a mom. And although I know no two families are the same, in most, that guy you fall asleep beside, share a bathroom with, and whose socks you fold is the guy who made you a mother. In other words . . .

Your kids only exist because you two got together.

Don't forget that! Those rascally, adorable, infuriating, loving, snuggly humans who make your heart want to burst with pride came into this world because you and your husband fell in love. That's something to celebrate over and over.

So I'm gonna say something that might sound kind of radical.

Your relationship with your husband should be the primary relationship in your household—not your relationship with your kids.

Shocking, maybe, but true. And you'll be a better mom for it, believe me. I would even put prioritizing and nurturing your marriage up there with self-care.

Think about it. Chances are, if you and your partner deliberately make time for each other, you'll be happier and feel more fulfilled. You'll probably also experience more joy, patience, and love with him. And do you think that will spill over into your relationship with your kids?

Oh yes, girlfriend.

And you know what else? You're setting a great example for them. You're teaching them what a loving, respectful relationship looks like. You only need to look at your own parents (for better or for worse) to understand how important that is.

Having been in a marriage where romance and date nights were not a priority, I know how fatal that lack of attention can be to a relationship. Remember what you and your spouse love about each other. Remember the reasons you got together, and hold on to those reasons. Celebrate them. Every. Single. Week.

The million-dollar question, of course, is how do you make it happen with kids to schlep to and from activities, feed, bathe, and, you know, *keep alive?*

First things first: talk about it!

If regular date nights with your spouse are not a thing in your marriage (yet), start off by having a conversation.

I'm no counselor, but I've loved enough to know that communication is key when it comes to relationships, and that's true whether we're talking about your relationship with your kids, your sister, your parents, or your best friend. Without a doubt, being open and up front with your husband is vital to prioritizing your marriage.

Second: plan!

You've gotta be intentional.

When you're planning your week, work in alone time for you and your significant other. Involve him in choosing the day of the week that would be best for both of you. Take turns deciding what you'll do on your date night. Make the process part of your time together.

And lastly, but super importantly, get help if you need it.

Shawn and I have what we like to call The Babysitter Optimizer.

We have five babysitters on rotation, all different ages and in different stages of their lives. We planned it that way strategically, so we won't lose everyone all at once when, say, it's time to go to college or time to get married. We're almost guaranteed that one of them will be available when we want some alone time away from home.

If a babysitter isn't your thing, rely on family. Grandparents love to see their grandkids!

And if help from family just isn't an option right now, for whatever reason, don't let that be your excuse. Sometimes Shawn and I do date nights at home, once our kiddos are in bed—or at the very least, upstairs with a movie (or, yes, a device).

The point is, you can make it happen. You might have to get creative or do a little finagling, but remember why you're doing it. Prioritizing your relationship is so important.

And mama, it's so worth it.

Chapter Seventeen

GO AHEAD AND ARGUE WITH YOUR SPOUSE (JUST USE THESE TIPS)

I get paid to fight with people.

Literally. As a commercial litigator, my job is to craft and deliver arguments about money (why my client should get it or shouldn't have to pay it) all day long. That back-and-forth exchange has taught me a lot over the years about how to argue effectively—and the golden nuggets I've picked up along the way have come in quite handy when it comes to disagreements with my husband.

I feel compelled to take a quick sidestep here and say that I absolutely adore my husband. He is my best friend and the love of my life. Our marriage is the second for both of us and—not to get all sappy and doe-eyed— we are straight up in love. I think the whole divorce thing equipped us each with a better screening process. Fifteen years, two kids, and one hellacious pandemic later, we're still totally into each other.

Hearts and flowers notwithstanding, however, my husband and I definitely argue. Heatedly, sometimes. After spending an entire year holed up together dealing with all the stresses that come with a global pandemic, it would be entirely unnatural if we didn't bicker. But, as a side effect of my occupational training, our arguments are (almost!) always productive.

Here's how to keep it loving and respectful when you're going head-to-head with your spouse.

Openly admit where your argument is weak—right out of the gate.

When presenting an argument to a judge, effective lawyers quickly concede the unfavorable facts on their side or whether law exists that could be interpreted against their position. Why?

For one, it builds credibility. Hiding bad facts—or worse, applicable law—to make you or your client look good will always backfire. And guess who's going to be caught in the midst of all that shrapnel? (Ahem. That would be *you*.)

Secondly, admitting where your argument is weak takes the bite out of any zingers your opponent was hoping to smack you with. Presenting a weakness before the other side can highlight it diminishes its perceived importance and its impact.

The same applies when you're arguing with your spouse. Being open about the ways in which you contributed to the dispute goes a long way toward building and fortifying trust. Plus, you'll appear rational, which means your spouse will actually listen to you.

For example, if my husband were to bite my head off in front of the kids for, say, dishonoring our budget and overspending at Athleta (hypothetically speaking, of course), my first words to him when it was appropriate to hash it out would be, "You're right about the budget. I should have been more conscious of what I was spending." And my very next words would be, "It is *not* OK to snap at me and it is *not* OK to do it in front of our kids."

Nine times out of ten, my admission of wrongdoing will completely diffuse his anger. Instead of trying to make me the bad guy, his objective will be to explain his viewpoint. He'll likely concede where he was wrong too, and then our shared objective will be to reconcile.

Beautiful how that works, isn't it?

Now, this is where I usually get the question, "But Nikki, what if I'm not wrong?"

To which I always reply, with a little bit of tough love, that in every argument, it takes two. You contribute to all conflicts you experience, and you play a role in everything that happens in your life—even the not so fun stuff. Once you can own that, things get a lot easier.

None of us is perfect, mama, not even you.

Use your inside voice.

I know when emotions are running high it's tempting to raise your voice, especially if you feel attacked or downright mad. But if there's one thing litigators don't do while presenting an argument, it's yell or name-call.

And with good reason. Decorum and professionalism aside, yelling to get your point across is not going to get you anywhere. The person on the receiving end won't be able to digest what you're saying because the sheer volume of your voice will put them into fight or flight mode. That's true whether you're speaking to opposing counsel, your kids, or your spouse.

While I'm a huge proponent of fully experiencing your emotions and feeling all the feels so you can release them (especially anger, hurt, and frustration), save the yelling for when it's not directed *at* the person with whom you share a duvet.

Don't try to win.

Unlike in the courtroom, there isn't supposed to be a clear winner when you and your significant other argue. Neither of you will walk away with a piece of paper that says "GRANTED" or "DENIED." No one is keeping score.

Truth? There is no "winning." At its core, an argument between two people who love each other is about communicating. It's about making sure the person on the other side understands where you're coming from and can acknowledge how you feel. The goal is to move past the disagreement with a better understanding of your partner and a blueprint for how you'd both handle a similar situation next time—not to declare yourself as "right" and the other person as "wrong."

Disagreements and debates are healthy in a relationship—no couple can agree about everything all the time. (How creepy would that be?) Just remember when you're having those spats that you're both human. You both want to be seen and heard.

So disagree, yes. Argue, yes. Then, get back to being on the same team and raising your beautiful humans *together*.

Chapter Eighteen

YOU'RE NEVER TOO OLD
TO TRY NEW THINGS

You know the adage, "You can't teach an old dog new tricks?" Do you ever feel like it sort of applies to you now that you're a mom with bills to pay and a house to take care of and humans who literally depend on you to live?

I'll admit I've had that thought a time or two since my days as a twenty-something (and yikes—even a thirty-something) are over. And yet, I long to learn new things.

One of my personal goals last year was to learn how to play chess. Or, more accurately, re-learn. It's a game I grew up playing sporadically when I'd visit my grandfather in South America, and one my dad and sister play well. Chess has been around forever—it's one of the oldest games in the world—and teaches you the skills of strategic and critical thinking. It also requires you to be completely present with your opponent as you play. That's one of the things I love most about it.

And I'll admit, *The Queen's Gambit* definitely had something to do with my renewed interest in the game.

Along the way, however, I've forgotten a lot of the rules. So, I decided last year that I'd pick it up again and re-teach myself. Lofty, right? I mean, it *sounded* good, but then I became paralyzed by the "how" of it.

"Who can teach me?"

"Are there resources online?"

"What's the first step in learning?"

I almost didn't even start, but then I recalled that my dad had bought a chess set for my kiddos and, along with it, a children's book on how to play.

So, I started there. With a children's book. It breaks the game down into easy-to-understand concepts intended to be consumed by a ten-year-old, and as it turns out, is a marvelous way for a crazy busy, not-twenty-and-not-even-thirty-anymore working mom of two to learn as well.

And let me tell you, girlfriend—it worked!

That got me thinking. Maybe learning something new by consuming the kid version first could be a thing. Why not?

By necessity, the kid version won't be complicated. It will be straight-forward, with examples that actually teach you the concept without trying to trick you, and will build slowly, one concept after another. Depending on the subject matter, the kid version might even gamify the learning process.

And did you ever notice that folks who started working on their craft when they were kids tend to be really good at them? Yes, they've been practicing for years. But I think there's also a correlation there with the *way* they learned.

Think of the possibilities! Sewing. Cake decorating. Scrapbooking. Cooking. Photography. Coding. Even sports.

After figuring out this new "kid trick," I asked my tennis coach to teach me how to improve my game by doing drills with me that he does with my daughter. "I don't care if it seems silly or pointless. I want to learn," I told him. He took me up on it, and I held true to my word, doing the drills that seemed like they were too simple to actually be teaching me anything, until one day, I realized we had completely transformed my swing through a series of small, fundamental, yet easy-to-implement changes.

You should see my forehand now, mama. It's pretty awesome, if I do say so myself.

So if you think you're an old dog who can't learn new tricks, I say hogwash! After all, anyone can do anything. Why not you?

Chapter Nineteen

ENTERTAINING YOUR KIDS FROM HOME WITHOUT LOSING YOUR MIND

I consider myself to be an awesome mom. I fully embrace my duty to protect my kids and harmonize that duty with my obligation to humanity to ensure they don't grow up to be jerks.

In alignment with my duty to protect them, I make sure my kiddos—much to their chagrin—don't eat junk. I insist they wear rash guards in the hot, South Florida sun. I cover them in sunscreen to the point that they look like snowmen (not kidding). When one of them gets angry and starts to throw a tantrum, I remind them it's OK to fully experience their feelings—as long as they don't hurt themselves, others, or my painstakingly decorated living room. Heartache and disappointment? I'm on it. Boo-boos? I got your back. Second-grade math homework and kindergarten reading? I'm your girl.

But when it comes to entertaining my kids from home, I'm a deer in headlights.

At least I *was*, until the great quarantine of 2020 forced me and every other mom in the world to figure out what the heck to do with our kids while we were all home together.

To my surprise, it was a huge blessing to be Director of Fun from Home (you like that title? I just made it up). It quickly taught me how to connect with my kids and share experiences with them that we otherwise might not have had if we weren't trying to make the most of it without playgrounds, arcades, restaurants, and trampoline entertainment centers.

And the best part? I didn't lose my mind!

Although I'm hopeful that quarantining is a thing of the past, this skill of entertaining kids from home is not one we should abandon. You just might need to whip it out again on the next snow day (or in my neck of the woods, the next hurricane day). Or perhaps you just want everyone in your house to get their faces away from their screens and have fun together this weekend while actually seeing each other's eyeballs.

Here are my tried-and-true tips for entertaining kids from home without losing your mind.

Get outside.

There is something so cleansing about fresh air. As busy people who live in paradise, my husband and I so often take it for granted. But what an amazing resource it is!

Go for a bike ride. Shoot some hoops or hit some tennis balls. Play catch in your yard. Take a run. Build a snowman (not that I'd know anything about that). Connecting with Mother Nature is so good for your soul. Plus, a little Vitamin D never hurt anyone. And bonus: running around outside will likely tire your kids out. Score!

Bake something yummy.

"No! I don't want to make delicious chocolate-chip cookies!" said no kid ever.

I don't know about your kids, but mine *love* to bake. They especially love it if they get to crack an egg. Grab your favorite recipe and whip up something delish! Not only will you get to teach your kids about measuring and how to follow a recipe (both great life skills), but you'll also get to eat brownies (or cake or cookies or muffins) when all is said and done. Winning!

Get your game on!

Whatever happened to good old-fashioned game night?

There's a reason games like Monopoly, Sorry!, Life, Mouse Trap, Twister, Uno, and Operation are still on the market. It's because they're still awesome! Let your inner child loose and bust out one of your old favorites. My kids fall over laughing hysterically when I play Twister with them. Add some popcorn to the mix, and you'll be golden.

Let them help you with something.

Kids love to feel useful. They especially love it when they feel like they're being trusted to do something only grown-ups do.

Let your kiddos help you wash your car, prepare a meal, or even fold and put away laundry. I'm always surprised by the chores and projects my kids want to help me with. Two birds with one stone? Yes, please.

Get crafty!

You don't have to be artsy to pull this one off.

Dust off that pencil box full of crayons and whip out the glue, scissors, and construction paper. Bonus if you have stickers, pom poms, or pipe cleaners. And if you're feeling really sassy, add some glitter to the mix. Pick a theme and get to creating.

Have beads and string? Make jewelry. Go nuts! You might find that you enjoy this one more than your kids!

Read together.

If your kiddos can read on their own, pick some quiet time to sit on the couch together and read your own books. (I recommend reading an actual book versus one on a device.)

If your kids are too young to read by themselves, read to them. My kids have been reading for years, but they still love it when I read to them, especially when I get into character. And I'll admit, I enjoy it too. (I always wanted to be an actress . . .)

Reading with your kids is so important. Not only is it great bonding time, but it's vital for their education. I remind my kids all the time that literally everything they want to do in life (including playing Minecraft) requires them to read. Might as well get good at it!

Channel your inner green goddess.

Teach your kids about nature by doing some work in your own yard. Pull weeds or water the plants. You could even do an experiment and plant seeds from fruit you have in your own kitchen. Boom! Science lesson.

Make stuff out of paper.

I don't know why, but kids love this stuff.

Paper airplanes, paper boats that actually float in water, and fortune tellers are top in my house. Don't know how to make any of these things? No problem. There is no shortage of tutorials on YouTube just waiting to instruct you.

Teach them the games you played as a kid.

Mansion Apartment Shack House (M.A.S.H.). Rock, paper, scissors. Hopscotch. Miss Mary Mack.

Remember those?

They were endlessly entertaining for us when we were little and they still are today. Plus they're totally free! A quick Google search will refresh your recollection if you've forgotten any of the lyrics or rules. And enjoy the trip down memory lane! It's sure to make you smile.

Chapter Twenty

GETTING STUFF DONE WHEN YOUR KIDS ARE HOME

Entertaining your kids from home is all fine and dandy if you can participate in the entertainment. But what are you supposed to do if you have to actually work while your kids are home with you?

These days, many moms now have the flexibility to work from home, which is an amazing benefit. But on a teacher planning day or when school is unexpectedly closed due to inclement weather, working from home can get tricky and downright frustrating, because—let's face it—the task of keeping the kiddos settled usually (almost always) falls on us.

Here's what works for me.

Wake up earlier.

As lovely as it would be to first roll out of bed whenever you happen to wake up naturally, if you want to get stuff done while your kids are home, you might have to rely on those wee hours of the morning.

The hours before the sun rises are the quietest and most productive of my day. I meditate, pray, and then get to work on anything that requires absolute focus and peace. No matter which industry you're in, you probably have some job tasks (like reading and deleting emails or doing paperwork) that can be completed during non-business hours.

You'll be shocked at how much you can get done when you're not hearing, "Mom? Mom? *Mom!*" every five seconds.

Tune into an online yoga or fitness class for kids.

If your kids are too young to read on their own, try getting their attention with an at-home phys-ed class.

You can find great classes for various age groups on YouTube. The yoga classes tend to be longer than the fitness ones, so keep that in mind when you're selecting one.

For younger kiddos, the yoga classes may be your best bet. They have themes ranging from Old McDonald to Frozen to Trolls. If you play your cards right, you should be able to get 15 to 25 minutes out of this trick.

Set up an art station.

This one is risky because of the high potential that paint, play-doh, or slime will permanently end up where it does not belong.

I've found, however, that covering my countertop in copious amounts of plastic wrap significantly mitigates that risk. If you can give them something structured like a figurine or a rock to paint, their concentration will likely last longer than it would if you just left them unattended to slap paint, markers, or crayons onto paper. I can usually buy myself 20 to 30 uninterrupted minutes with this trick.

Warning: Do *not* leave them alone with glitter. Don't do it. Glitter is like the herpes of the craft world. You cannot get rid of it. You will find it lurking in remote corners of your home for years to come.

Make the most of nap time.

If your kids still nap, this time might be the only time you can squeeze in some work—maybe even a conference call. If you can couple this time with waking up earlier, you should be able to make a meaningful dent in your workload.

Allow them to watch a movie.

Sometimes, mama's gotta rely on Disney.

Thankfully, there are a ton of great options on the Disney+ app. Choose something you and your kiddos all find acceptable and give them some popcorn. If you can, set up your work station close enough so you can intervene if they start trying to kill each other.

Depending on how old your kids are and how entertaining the movie is, this option should give you at least 45 minutes.

Let them get on a device.

It's not ideal, but when you've gotta get something done, it's your best bet.

There are some great educational apps that kids actually enjoy, like PBS Kids and ABC Mouse, and some awesome educational websites your kids are sure to love, like *Seussville* or *Fun Brain*. Or you could let them watch National Geographic Kids or Brain Pop, Jr. on YouTube, or do a video chat with a classmate.

Whatever you decide, just know it's OK. On some days, in some moments, it's just about survival. An hour on the iPad when you need to be on a call or focus on getting something submitted is truly not the worst thing in the world.

Be patient.

Let your employer know when your kiddos are unexpectedly home for the day. After everything we went through in 2020, most will adjust their expectations because they remember what it's like. No mom can be sitting in front of her computer for hours at a stretch while her kids are awake.

Give yourself a *ton* of grace.

Remember that you are already amazing and you're doing the best you can. You don't have to be perfect, girlfriend.

Chapter Twenty-One

THE ROAD YOU'RE ON

When my husband and I got married, we went on a spectacular honeymoon.

I'll always remember how glorious it felt on our wedding night to walk into our honeymoon suite after the reception and settle into the splendid reality that I would be doing zero lawyering for two weeks in favor of wine tasting for five days in Napa Valley, followed by seven days of utter relaxation in Maui, Hawaii.

By the way, have you ever been to Maui? It totally deserves all the hype. Truly, with its exotic flowers, native traditions, and awe-inspiring landscapes, it's like being in a different country—only like, super comfortable, because of the whole dollar-accepting, English-speaking, U.S. Constitution-abiding thing.

Leading up to our visit, we repeatedly heard from folks at home and in Napa alike, "You must take the road to Hana when you get to Maui." So when we checked in at the Grand Wailea a few days later and our concierge made the same recommendation, we knew we had to do it.

We rented a Jeep, got a map and some bottled water, and set out on the trek to Hana, just two excited newlyweds up for an adventure. We were told to set aside an entire day for the trip and were given recommendations for places to stop along the way.

We visited Kuau Cove to watch powerful blue-green waves crash over and over again on the shore. We hiked in flip flops through thigh-deep water to reach a breathtaking waterfall and swam in the freezing cold lagoon it poured into. We walked barefoot along the beach at the Waianapanapa Caves, letting our toes sink into the black sand, dark from volcanic sediment and ash. We explored a real lava tube in pitch-black darkness with only the flashlights in our hands to guide us.

And then, at long last, we reached our destination.

Hana, as it turned out, was fairly nondescript. I sort of don't even remember it. There was a visitor center, I think. And maybe a koi pond? I'm sure in isolation it's beautiful, perhaps even breathtaking. I mean, it's in Maui after all. But after the incredible journey we'd just experienced, arriving at our destination was sort of... meh.

That was more than 12 years ago. It's not often I think about our honeymoon now, with the day-to-day bustle of raising two kids, running a household, lawyering, aspiring to be an amateurish tennis champion, and building a business to consume my being and doing.

But the other day, I was reading something that mentioned the road to Hana and I thought, *Hey, I've done that!*

The author described the many sites along the famous route and warned that if you simply drove straight through them in an effort to get to Hana quickly, you would actually miss the whole point of taking the road to Hana in the first place. I nodded in agreement as I read. After all, people don't tell you to visit Hana. They tell you to *take the road* to Hana.

You know where I'm going with this, right? It's about the journey, not the destination. After taking the road to Hana, I understand this saying physically and experientially.

But when it comes to motherhood, I often forget I'm on a journey. It doesn't register when I'm in Target wrangling my kids, stopping them from trying to murder each other by threatening to murder them myself, and an older woman smiles knowingly at me and says, "Enjoy it, honey." Always, I smile back politely, but it's all I can do not to shake my head and say, "Enjoy *this?!* You cray, lady!"

It doesn't register in other parts of my life either, like when my tennis coach, after witnessing me hit ball after ball into the net and then over the fence—whilst groaning and stifling blood-curdling screams—encourages me to "enjoy the process" of improving my tennis game. *Enjoy sucking?!* I think, before demanding out loud to know when I'm going to start seeing results.

And it definitely does not register when I'm enduring each phase of growing my business. I don't really hear my mentor when she tells me that this is the hardest but most exciting time of entrepreneurship, when I'm throwing spaghetti at the wall to see what will stick, learning what to do and what not to do.

No. I'm too focused on getting to a time when my kids are bigger and better behaved, when my forehands skid off the baseline and don't come back, when my podcast has one million downloads.

I'm focused on getting to Hana.

Oops. (Cue palm smacking into forehead now.) Damn, what have I been missing out on? Did I already drive by the black sand beach and the lava tube? Did I miss the waterfall?

Talk about a total paradigm shift.

Seeing the process in that light turns it into something else entirely. The journey isn't something to complain about. It's something to be *enjoyed*. Photographed, memorialized, scrapbooked, even!

I'd venture to say the same is true for you. Where do you find yourself squandering the journey in favor of the destination? On your way to becoming debt-free? Or losing 25 pounds? Or earning a promotion at work? Perhaps it's surviving this time of being home with two kids under two (or even three under three!).

Whatever it is, don't be so focused on getting to where you're going that you miss experiencing the unthinkable miracles and opportunities surrounding you along the way.

Enjoy the road you're on, girlfriend. It's beautiful. And so is who you're becoming in the process.

Chapter Twenty-Two

DEALING WITH CHANGE WHEN YOUR KIDS ARE WATCHING

Change is the great equalizer. Whether we like it or not, all of us are going to experience change in our lives.

I believe no one understands this concept better than a mama. Remember life (and your body) before your first baby? Yeah, things have definitely changed since then.

And like everything in life, change involves duality. Sometimes change is good—like having a baby, scaling your business to the next level, earning a promotion, or discovering a new ice cream flavor.

And sometimes change can feel . . . not as good. Especially when we don't feel we chose it. Losing a loved one. Moving to a foreign place. Breaking up with a significant other or losing a job.

But often, change that feels not so good is actually greatness hiding inside some icky discomfort.

Like an edamame bean. You have to bite through a weird, hairy shell that's way too hard to swallow to get to the good stuff.

So what are we supposed to do with that when change pops up in our lives? How do we embrace the icky discomfort so we can get to the good—especially when our kids are watching us?

I faced this challenge recently, and it dawned on me during an early morning meditation that I should probably start with doing as I say.

That probably doesn't make any sense. Lemme back up.

I do affirmations with my kids. It occurred to me one day when they were really little that someday, in the distant future, mean kids might tell my adorable, sweet, innocent little babies that they're dumb. Or weird. Or bad at sports. You know—the stuff You-Can't Monsters are made of. And in that moment of realization, I actually felt offended and mad. I was all, *"Aw, heck no!"* (Please tell me I'm not the only woman who goes mama bear over situations that haven't even happened yet.)

Anyhoo, the whole experience got me thinking . . . how can I prepare them for the inevitable trials of youth and adolescence—for the mean girls and the merciless boy hazing? How do I prepare them for the stuff beyond all that, like the scariness of choices and trying something new and putting yourself out there?

I settled on affirmations.

And so, since they were small, I have told them every day, "You are smart, kind, and important. You can do hard things. You don't give up easily." As they got bigger, we added a few to the list, like "I try new things." Admittedly, I threw that one in there so I could waggle a finger at them when they wrinkled their noses at new foods and be like, "Remember! We try new things!"

But when you're experiencing a change, those words take on new meaning. That's what I meant earlier when I said I should do as I say.

At its core, the discomfort that surrounds a change that's been forced upon us is always rooted in fear.

We're afraid the new won't be as good as the old. We're afraid we won't be able to handle it. We're afraid we might suffer, be embarrassed, or feel pain.

But you know what? There was once a time when you had never before tasted ice cream or coffee. You might even have been *afraid* to taste them at first. But you tried those new things anyway. And look at your life now! Can you imagine your life without coffee? (Side note: I gave up caffeine a few years ago, so I actually *can* imagine my life without coffee, but substitute your vice here. Wine. Botox. TikTok. Whatever.)

A bit tongue-and-cheek? Maybe. But I think, at the end of the day, the analysis is the same with any change.

Our fear is blocking our growth.

Don't get me wrong. I'm not saying you should always ignore your fear. We were created with those instincts for a reason, and although it's been a while since anyone has seen a saber-toothed tiger, honoring your fear does still come in handy in serious situations.

I *am* saying that giving in to fear merely to stay comfortable means you won't give yourself rich new experiences that help you grow.

What if you try that new food and it's delish? What if losing that old job helps you discover a passion you can parlay into a new career that lights you up? What if you move to that new city and you love it?

Be open to those "what ifs." Remember that God and the universe are always working everything together for your good. Don't hold yourself back from experiencing that good, even when it's forced on you and has taken the form of a hard, hairy bean you've never seen before.

You know, to this day, my kids and I always end our affirmations with, "I'm brave. I'm powerful."

And you are, girlfriend. You are.

Chapter Twenty-Three

HATERS GONNA HATE

No family is perfect.

I think we all know this inherently, but was I the only mom in America who was kind of relieved a couple of years ago to get certain confirmation from Oprah's famous interview with Harry and Meghan that even the *Royal* Family has issues?

No matter what you thought of the interview, I think we can all relate to bits of what the former Duchess of Sussex shared. I know I'm not world-famous, and I understand that I'm not being watched by the British media (or, um, any media, for that matter) as they plot ways to assassinate my character before the nation, while my majestic in-laws look on smiling. That's not the part of this story I find relatable. But hasn't anyone ever treated you unfairly or said things about you that were completely false?

When my husband and I first started dating, he was navigating this weird, financial dynamic with his family. As the first to graduate from high school, then college, and then graduate school, he was expected by his parents and siblings alike to pay for them when they got together for family events—even if the event was his own birthday. If one of them fell behind on a bill, his phone would ring.

They weren't even grateful. They expected it.

It was clear to me as an outsider that his family didn't want to acknowledge the truth, which was that he had built himself up from scratch. He had busted his ass to pay his tuition and pass his exams, and even as a full-blown professional he never stopped hustling.

With that truth came a hard pill to swallow: they could do it too, if they worked hard enough. It was much easier for them to believe he was simply "lucky" and that he suddenly "got rich."

So they held their hands out instead. And my husband, for his part, forked it over.

By the time I came into the picture, he was sick and tired of that dance. Realizing that he had been complicit in their behavior by stepping in time to the music for so long, he slowly, deliberately changed the moves. He started to push back. He asked his family to pay their portions of the bill at restaurants. He refused to give them money willy-nilly.

And let me tell you: they did *not* like it.

Unfortunately for me, my husband changed his tune right around the inception of our relationship. And his family, not believing for one second that he could have grown so defiant on his own, chose to blame me.

So yeah, that was a fun way to start things off.

For months, they whispered behind my back about how I wouldn't "let" my husband-then-boyfriend give them money (false) because I had gotten him his "cushy" job working for a global conglomerate financial institution through my law firm (false) and felt entitled to tell him how to spend his paycheck. False, false, false. Mind you, however, no one had the guts to say any of that nonsense to my face, or to his.

And then he asked me to marry him.

It wasn't until my bridal shower, when none of the women of his family bothered to show up, that I became crushingly aware they harbored such ill feelings toward me. I was devastated.

That's when it all came out—everything they had been saying and had believed about me that wasn't true. And I'm not gonna lie. I didn't take it well. I felt victimized and betrayed. I was angry at the unfairness of it all.

And although my husband was fuming at his family and very squarely in my corner, I felt alone.

What I eventually learned from that experience is that it is vital in those moments to know who you are. But like, really know it, deep in your core.

You're kind. You're smart. You're important. You can do hard things. You don't give up easily.

When you know those things about yourself, no one can take them away from you. When you truly know who you are, you can center yourself in that certainty to draw strength. No matter what anyone else says about you.

Listen, girlfriend, people are probably going to hate on you at some point in your life. Maybe they'll be other moms who envy that you're putting yourself out there and want to put you down to feel better about themselves. Maybe they'll be your own family. Being certain about who you are doesn't necessarily make it hurt less. But it does make it easier to see your choices.

We get to decide what we do with those experiences. We get to choose if we're going to find the lesson and allow it to make us stronger.

How we show up for ourselves is completely up to us.

More than a decade and two kids later, my in-laws and I get along better than I ever thought possible. My husband addressed the elephant in the room, set them straight, and we haven't looked back since.

OK, fine.

Every once in a blue moon, I do look back. But I'm clear now on why I created that experience and what I took from it. I'm grateful for it, because it revealed a blind spot and gave me an opportunity to grow immensely.

We *all* get those opportunities.

The next time you get one, remember who you are.

Choose to find the lesson in the hurt and to absorb the strength that comes with experiencing it.

Chapter Twenty-Four

WHAT TO DO WHEN THE MEAN GIRLS ATTACK

When I became a legit adult—complete with my own home, car, checking account, and fancy career—I thought all of that petty stuff I experienced as a teenage girl was behind me. You know what I mean. The cliques and the drama and the cat-fighting that are often the hallmarks of a woman's adolescence.

And then . . . I became a mom.

Yeah, in theory we're all adults, but sometimes in real life it can feel like we're still in high school.

Not so long ago, a fellow grown-up was mean to me. On purpose. Hiding behind the anonymity the internet provides, she harshly criticized something I had created without providing any real feedback or basis for her opinion. She just wanted to hate on me, I guess. And it reminded me that those mean girls from high school are still around, and they're still, well . . . mean.

Mean girl attacks happen all the time when you really think about it.

Nasty reviews, rude comments on Facebook or Instagram, mom-shaming—these are all modern-day ways the mean girls attack. In my neck of the woods, two moms went at it with each other in federal court, over a dispute that started on the tennis court. (I can't even make this stuff up.) So what do you do when the mean girls attack you?

Here's what my mean-girl slashings have taught me.

Experience your feelings.

Let's be real. It sucks when someone is mean to you.

But as much as we'd all like to feel sunshine and butterfly kisses every day, the reality is that experiencing our lows is just as important as experiencing our highs. Truly, we couldn't appreciate the good if we never experienced anything bad.

So when someone is mean to you, be honest with yourself about how it feels. It's OK if you feel crappy about it. Don't try to stuff, resist, or push those feelings aside. And definitely don't distract yourself from feeling them. (Side note: lying to yourself is never a good thing.) Plus, as a friend and mentor once told me, pretending to be happy when you're not is like painting over rust. The rust is still there, my friend.

Try a healthier and more productive approach: give yourself a moment to fully *feel*. Feel the anger, disappointment or hurt. Cry it out. Just remember that you get to decide how long you stay in that space. My advice? Experience the emotion full-out and then let it go.

After my brush with the anonymous mean girl, I definitely felt like someone had slapped me. I won't lie. I wallowed for a few hours in "I'm not good enough," and "No one likes me," and "Why am I even trying?"

And then . . . I let it go. I chose to remember the absolute truth—that what someone thinks of me doesn't change who I am. It definitely doesn't dictate my future. I've got a lot to offer this world, and mark my words: I'm gonna.

And you know what, girlfriend? So are you.

Find the lesson.

Listen, as cliché as it sounds, there's a lesson in every experience. It's our job to find it. And not only for our own sakes, but so we can guide our kids when this stuff happens to them. Because you know it will.

In my case, I learned a lot from my reaction. I realized how much importance I put on being good at what I do—*and on getting validation from others* that I'm good at what I do. I was desperate to know why the mean girl rated my work so poorly so I could rationalize her opinion or defend myself in my own mind. The fact that she didn't give me the satisfaction was bitterly disappointing.

But it also helped me to remember not all criticism is created equal. Sometimes people criticize you because they're truly trying to help you improve, or, at the very least, want you to do better.

Other times, they just wanna give you the finger.

My run-in with the mean girl was a great reminder that I can't please everyone. Not everything I do or say is going to resonate with everyone, and that's OK. (No, really, it is OK.) Let's not ignore the majority of people who love and value you in favor of giving power and attention to the one who doesn't.

I was also reminded not to make up stories in my head about why other people do the things they do. When people don't respond to your text messages or call you back; when they ignore your emails; when they give you bad ratings online, unfriend or unfollow you, don't think for one second that you *actually* know why. In most cases, it ain't got nothin' to do with you.

And let's not forget, some girls are just crabs in a bucket. They want to pull you down and keep you from rising up because they can't stand the thought of someone else doing well. They just don't believe they can shine if you do too. Is that your problem?

Nope.

Another thing I learned is that if I'm going to stick it out as a person who creates content to help other moms love their mom lives (and I fully intend to), I have to get used to people having opinions about what I create, and opinions that won't always be complimentary. Most of the time, their opinions won't even give me much to go on. I have to draw on my own strength and self-worth to keep going. As one of my best friends said to me after the fact, weapons cannot be strong unless they move through intense heat and pressure. These bumps in my journey are applying heat and pressure to make me stronger.

Same goes for you, my friend. Unpleasant experiences are opportunities to grow. Plain and simple.

Finally, this whole thing taught me that I've probably been the mean girl to someone else. And chances are, so have you. Remember how it feels to be on the receiving end next time you're tempted to dish it out. I know I will.

Give yourself the win.

Just like there's a lesson in every experience, there's also (almost always) something good you can create from it too. Why not divert your energy and propel yourself into action? In my case, the mean-girl experience resulted in this chapter!

Next time you endeavor to be open and honest about who you are and what you have to offer, ask yourself, "How can I create something worth criticizing?" For real. Give yourself the win. Honestly, if you're doing something that other people are bothering to criticize, you're doing something right.

Putting yourself out there, whether you're running your own business, crushing it as a leader in your organization, or serving others in any way, is *hard*. It is not easy to wear your heart on your sleeve and literally bear your soul to the public at the risk of them trampling all over it.

But keep doing it.

Keep showing up. Keep giving it your all. Keep believing that you can do anything. Because you know what? You can.

Chapter Twenty-Five

IT'S OK TO NOT EVEN TRY SOMETIMES

I go for stuff.

I'm not the girl who sits around waiting for life to happen to her. I don't complain about so-called "bad luck" or hate on other people's success. No way. I believe we create everything we experience in life and, with God as my source, I step into my power and I go for stuff.

That's not to say I don't suffer from attacks of imposter syndrome (or as I like to call it, the You-Can't Monster). To be very clear, I'm a big fan of the ugly cry on a rough day.

So in early 2020 when I signed up to do a Spartan "sprint" (which, mind you, is several miles of hell, complete with 21 obstacles, barbed wire, and a lot of mud), I thought, *OK. I'm gonna go for this.*

But then the pandemic happened and the race was postponed. My Hard Exercise Works gym, where many a Spartan athlete is born, was forced to temporarily close. We all stayed home for several tumultuous months, and I eventually fell out of doing my crazy-hard workouts. And when the race was finally rescheduled, it all felt a lot less . . . fun, I guess, to the extent getting filthy while voluntarily enduring pain in the name of fitness ever seemed *fun.*

But because I'm the girl who goes for stuff, I also tend to be very, very hard on myself. I do not let myself off the hook easily. And I've been known to berate myself when I feel I've underperformed or not shown up the way I thought I should.

Thus, twenty-four hours before the race began, I found myself in an intense debate. With . . . myself.

"You said you were going to do it, so you should do it."

I nodded. "Yeah. I should just do it." I wrinkled my nose. "But I really don't want to."

"Yeah, but you'll be stronger for it. You'll definitely grow."

"I know I will." I sighed. "But I really don't want to."

I intermittently had this back-and-forth conversation with myself all day. Finally, when my bestie and fellow Spartan texted me to find out what I had decided, I wrote back, "I guess I should just do it."

She responded, "Or you could not do it and be OK with it."

Wait. What?

Picture that moment in rom-coms where the protagonist has an epiphany and the music swells, the lighting gets brighter, and the camera swoops in.

Yes! I thought. *I could just not do it and be OK with it. Yes!*

So that's what I did. I took myself out of the race before I even laced up my shoes. I quit. I didn't even try.

And damn, girlfriend, it felt *gooood.*

It felt so good to give myself permission to do exactly what I wanted, even if that meant I wasn't going to do something I had signed up for.

It was quite a foreign experience. Remember, I'm the girl who goes for stuff.

So as that girl, I have to make sure you don't get me wrong.

I'm not saying it's OK to flippantly bail on your commitments. It is not cool to leave people hanging when they're depending on you to show up. I'm not saying you should start things and not finish them. And I am definitely not saying it's OK to make excuses when the going gets tough.

Because, duh, if we constantly did that, we'd never accomplish our big, hairy, audacious goals. We wouldn't learn how to do new things. We'd never grow. And we'd never be able to expect our kids to either.

What I *am* saying is that when your heart's not in it, when you're not doing it for the right reasons, when no one else is going to be put out, it's OK to give yourself a break.

In my case, my bestie had already done two Spartan races and had made it very clear to me she felt no qualms about skipping this one. I, on the other hand, had not been training for it. In fact, I was dreading it. My heart just wasn't in it.

And that's why giving myself a break on this one was the most loving thing I could have done for myself.

All you perfectionists out there, all you mamas who are so hard on yourselves, who never, ever let yourself off the hook—let that sink in. *It's OK to give yourself a break.* Giving yourself a break can be the deepest form of self-care. Truly, it's an act of love.

Next time you're faced with forcing yourself to do something you really don't want to do, and that truly won't hurt you to skip, ask yourself: Is my heart in this? Am I doing this for the right reasons? Is anyone else's life going to be more difficult if I decide not to follow through?

If the answer to those questions is no, skip it. Give yourself the break. Trust yourself and allow yourself to receive all the beautiful blessings that flow your way when you do.

Take the win that comes with loving yourself enough to know when you need to take care of you.

Chapter Twenty-Six

....

WHEN YOU FALL
OFF THE WAGON

Have you ever been totally rocking something—like you were showing up every day, doing the work, looking in the mirror saying, "Consistency is my middle name!"—and then completely fallen off the wagon?

Maybe for you it was eating well and exercising as you worked toward a weight loss goal. Perhaps you were on a meditation streak, or you were honoring your morning routine and faithfully making time just for you.

In my case, it was all those things because I had consistently been time blocking my weeks and owning my days.

Until suddenly, I wasn't.

It happened so slowly that even now, as I deliberately reflect on what went wrong, I can't pinpoint when it began. One day I noticed I wasn't waking up as early as I had intended, which meant I wasn't honoring my morning routine. That, in turn, meant I wasn't meditating, praying, or journaling on a regular basis, nor was I working on my biggest professional goal.

It also meant my exercise equipment got dusty, my knives, cutting boards, and pans went unused in favor of takeout, and the laundry situation in my household became utterly dire.

I found I wasn't owning my time at all. I was allowing other people to dictate what I did and when I did it, instead of honoring my priorities and setting boundaries to protect my glass balls. I was getting sucked into what seemed urgent but, upon reflection, wasn't actually *important*.

On Sundays, when I looked back on the week I'd just had, I realized I hadn't touched many of the things that support *my* life's goals, the things that fill me up and make me feel like I'm making a massive impact on the world.

And then shit finally hit the fan.

I landed a speaking engagement for the women's initiative of a very prestigious law firm. The audience was female lawyers and the topic was burnout which, as an expert, I know is caused almost entirely by struggles with time management. The moderator of the event and I scheduled a time to hop on Zoom to prepare, but because I had been spread so thin and had become so out of practice with time blocking, *I missed the call.*

Yeah. That happened.

And although she was the epitome of grace and we rescheduled and smoothed everything out, I realized (after bursting into tears and momentarily indulging the part of me that wanted to wallow and feel like a total fraud and a complete failure) that there was only one way to get out of this rut I had fallen into.

I needed to get back to practicing what I preach.

The point of this rather embarrassing story is twofold. First, I want you to understand that even those of us who literally wrote the book on this subject can fall off the wagon and find ourselves once again on the Hot Mess Express. Take comfort in knowing that no one is perfect at this stuff. We working mamas are all in this together, and we all have opportunities for growth.

Second, this experience has shown me in real time how incredibly important it is to plan your days and honor your plans, and precisely how quickly things can spiral into chaos when you don't. The beauty of having fallen down is that I got to pick myself back up and share with you how you can too if you were ever to find yourself in this situation (hypothetically speaking, of course).

Here's how to get back on the horse.

Identify what most likely derailed you.

In my case, it was saying yes when I should have been saying no (politely, of course).

I had taken on this false belief that I could successfully bite off more than I could chew. I knew better, and yet I did it anyway, and the result was exactly what you would expect.

Remember that time invested in one area is time away from another. If it's not your best yes, *don't say yes.*

By saying "no," you're creating an opportunity for someone else to shine and give *her* best yes. It really is that simple.

So next time you're faced with having to say no, say it. Be powerful enough to be honest. And if saying no on the spot feels too scary, you can always ask for time to give it some thought and get back to them. Give yourself some time to think, pray, or feel about it, come up with kind but honest words to use, and then get back to that person and just say no.

Sometimes saying no to others is the only way to say yes to yourself.

Make a "to-don't" list.

I wholeheartedly encourage you to go *nuts* with this.

Indulge the tantrums of your inner child and emphatically say no to every single thing you just do not want to do. Lay it all out there on the paper and be brutally honest.

Even if in the end, you truly must keep some of those things on your list, admitting you don't want to do them anymore will prompt you to figure out a way to make them less taxing by outsourcing help or implementing a new system.

Purge the clutter from your mind.

When my mind is cluttered with every single thing I need to get done from every area of my multi-faceted life, from lawyering to momming to volunteering for the PTA, I feel crippled by overwhelm. And when I pause to think about it, I realize I feel like I'm drowning because I haven't been doing a regular mental dump.

Take it from me: the mental dump is vital. And it's ridiculously easy. All you have to do is jot down every single "to-do" item weighing on your mind. Just get it out of your head and onto paper.

I'm talking *everything*, my friend. It doesn't matter what area of your life it pertains to. It doesn't matter if it's big or small. It doesn't matter how long it's been on your list. It doesn't matter if you think you'll never have time to do it. If it's on your mind, dump it onto the paper.

Once it's all out and captured in one place, it can be sorted, prioritized, and *(ta da!)* cross-referenced against your to-don't list.

And girl, let me tell you. Getting it out feels so good.

Remember what it is you truly want.

I'm certain my derailment occurred because I hadn't been focusing on what I want.

And the only way to truly manage your time and own your day when you're a working mom is to be certain about what you want out of life.

I realized that because I wasn't giving attention to what I want, I wasn't taking the right action, and because I wasn't taking proper action, I wasn't manifesting what I want. Instead, I spun around in circles every week (which, by the way, I have never enjoyed, not even on the teacups at Disney World).

So I chose to regain clarity, and if you're in this boat with me, I'm encouraging you to do the same.

Figure out from a "big picture" perspective what your personal and professional goals are. I recommend having a maximum of three annual goals for both your personal and professional lives. As we discussed in Chapter Three, once you know what those are, you can back into what you need to accomplish on a monthly, weekly, and daily basis to achieve those goals, and prioritize those items on your calendar.

Which brings me to my final tip.

Use your calendar!

This part is easy. You just need to remember the key to prioritizing and that the most important items should be blocked on your calendar first.

Understanding that not everything matters equally and that the balls representing the major areas of your life are made of either rubber or glass makes prioritizing a breeze. Quite simply, the glass balls must come first.

By this point in the process, you've already surveyed what's on your plate (the mental dump), what you're scraping off of it (your to-don't list), and what's most important to you. Now, all you have to do is calendar it.

And spoiler alert: it's not all going to fit into this week. But that's OK.

We are still crushing it and still on track because we are focusing on what matters most.

We all have setbacks. We all fall down or get knocked off course. The key is owning it so we can dust ourselves off and get back up.

Chapter Twenty-Seven

APPRECIATE THE DOORS
THAT SLAM IN YOUR FACE

I once asked hundreds of moms what their greatest daily challenge is.

The response, hands down, was not having enough time. That didn't surprise me in the least. You get it. You're probably nodding your head right now like, "*Girrrl*, ain't nobody more crunched for time than a mama."

Yet so often, we engage in colossal wastes of time and don't even realize we're doing it. There are the obvious time suckers, like doing for yourself what others can do for you or spinning in frenzied circles every morning when some simple planning and organization tricks could have you sailing smoothly (and quickly) out the door.

But there are also silent, sneaky thieves of our time. We can't see them, can't even pinpoint them, but they rob us of precious moments and keep us from fully enjoying life.

One such thief takes the form of doors that close in our faces.

Have you ever been dumped or fired and refused to let go? Or been unwilling to forgive yourself for something you wish you had handled differently with your kids or your husband? Even now, might you be holding on to how your body looked and felt before you had kids or to what "would have been" if the pandemic had never happened?

This might be a harsh truth, but pining away for what could have been is the ultimate waste of time.

I'm going to say something obvious because sometimes you (and I) need reminders: there is nothing you can do to change something that has already happened. Nothing. (Unless, of course, you have a time machine.)

Listen, I'm not saying you should dance around in glee when things don't work out. It's absolutely OK to be disappointed and hurt. And more importantly, it's OK to express that you're disappointed or hurt.

As with everything in life, though, you have a choice.

You get to decide how long you want to stay in a space of anger, sadness, or hurt. Experience it fully, you must, but once you do, realize that choosing to hold on to it or wishing it had gone down differently is not only a giant waste of time, but it's robbing you of the joy that has popped up in its place.

And yes, joy *has* popped up in its place. You only have to turn your head and see it.

It's like that famous quote from Alexander Graham Bell, "When one door closes, another opens; but we often look so long and so regretfully upon the closed door that we do not see the one which has opened for us." I wonder, friend . . . do you find yourself still staring at the door that the pandemic, or a diagnosis, or a former boss, or an ex-husband slammed in your face instead of at the door that's been opened for you through which you might find joy, peace, or healing?

My first marriage ended less than a year after it started. After five years of living together, we lasted eight measly months as husband and wife. For my part, it was humiliating and heartbreaking. I would stare at my wedding photos and feel like an idiot. I would go to friends' engagement parties convinced that everyone secretly pitied me for being such a loser. When I resumed using my maiden name, I thought I was literally going to die when everyone in my office received a new phone list with my name appearing in a different place alphabetically.

I felt unlovable. I felt like a complete and total failure. And you better believe I wasted hours upon *hours* wishing I had done things differently, that I could have avoided the hurt and the ugly I experienced in the months leading up to and after our divorce.

It took me years to appreciate that door slamming in my face. Now I can see it for what it was: a blessing. My only regret is that I wasted any time at all wishing it had never happened. Had it not, I would never have been able to walk through the door that opened for me almost immediately, which led me to the father of my children and the greatest love of my life.

Which begs the question: if there are unexpected blessings when doors are slammed in our faces, could we find similar fortune by closing some doors ourselves?

I'm voting yes.

Be grateful for the doors in your life that slam shut. Appreciate that God has made clear to you the closed door isn't the one you're supposed to walk through. And the open door? It might just be behind you, where you're not looking. Don't stare at the closed one for so long that you forget to turn around and see it.

Oh, and while you're at it, go ahead and shut those doors you should have closed a long time ago but left open. You're making the air conditioner work twice as hard, girlfriend.

Chapter Twenty-Eight

WHEN LIFE THROWS YOU A STORM

You've seen *Moana*, right?

Well, even if you haven't, or you have no idea who I'm talking about because your little humans have somehow never forced you to repeatedly watch Disney movies, stay with me. This is good stuff.

There's a part in the movie when Moana is out on the ocean, lost and alone, searching for a demi-god named Maui no one has seen in, like, hundreds of years. She has absolutely no idea how she's going to find him, having set sail with only a seashell necklace and an idiot chicken to guide her (ya gotta love Disney). And so, in a moment of desperate faith, she calls on the ocean for help.

The ensuing result is a tumultuous storm that tosses her and her tiny raft from wave to giant wave while she hangs on for her life in terror. The next morning, she finds herself shipwrecked on an island, frazzled and disoriented and seemingly no closer to finding Maui. Furious, she curses the ocean for toying with her, adding at the end of her assault, "Fish *pee* in you! *All day!*"

But in the next moment, who does she discover that just happens to be stranded on that island too?

Maui. The ocean delivered her *right* to him.

Wow. Did anyone else feel that metaphor like a two-by-four smack in the face? What a powerful illustration of real life.

Sometimes the fastest way to get from where you are to where you need to be is through a total shitstorm.

Think about it. Haven't you ever been through an awful situation, only to realize months or years later that it was "a blessing in disguise?" (Um, of course you have.)

Reflecting on my own life, I can see clearly—years and years later—that my divorce from my first husband was one of those storms, intended to take me from a toxic relationship into an ideal one. One in which fairytale romance is *real*. One in which passion does not wane. One in which God is ever-present. One that produced two children who are living, breathing manifestations of our intense love for one another.

And since then, it has also become clear that I *asked* for the storm, just like Moana did. I didn't realize it at the time, of course (who ever does?). But I can't deny it was indeed my own, unconscious creation. I like to think of it as my true self reaching out her hand and saying, *Come on, girlfriend. I know a shortcut. Just don't let go of my hand 'cause this is gonna get ugly.*

So when it happens to you, remember that you're taking a shortcut. Settle in and relax into the storm by staying present with every single wave. Don't resist it, don't curse it. Don't shut your eyes and wish it wasn't happening. Obviously, you created it because you need to experience it. After all, it's taking you exactly where you want to go.

With the benefit of hindsight and some self-discovery training, I'm able to see that it was silly to wish my ex-husband and I had never met, as I once used to. There was a time when I was desperate to erase us, when I wished I could have avoided the pain and humiliation of making what seemed like such a grave mistake.

But now I know all that wishing was wasted energy. The pain and humiliation I experienced had immense value. I learned who I am and what I can give myself. I learned what I can *take* from life.

And I want that for you. Once you can appreciate the storm, you can appreciate the good that washes ashore with it.

My ex-husband encouraged me to put myself through law school. The raw and simple truth is that I would never have gone if it weren't for him. At 23 years old, I believed my parents would pay for my tuition, and when they told me they couldn't, I thought that was simply the end of that. But not him. He helped me see I could do it myself, and that decision changed the trajectory of my entire life.

I'm grateful for the storms in my life now. I know they were designed to make me stronger and more powerful.

Oh, and speaking of power, did you ever notice how every superhero *always* has to overcome some kind of adversity on their way to becoming great? Dead parents, lost love, kidnapped children, terrorism, war—the list of tragedies is endless. You never read about a superhero who had zero problems and a cushy life filled with love. Nope, and you never will. They must endure the storm first.

Listen, I'm not saying your life should be some constant, painful grind. You should strive to create freedom, flow, and joy, always. But when you hit your stuff along the way, especially as you're mothering, remember The *Moana* Principle.

And while you're intentionally riding out the storm, remember that you got this, girlfriend.

Bet you never knew a Disney movie could be so deep, huh?

Chapter Twenty-Nine

CREATING A SENSE OF NORMALCY WHEN YOUR WORLD FLIPS UPSIDE DOWN

I can honestly say that I have never experienced more chaos in my entire life than I did when the world shut down in 2020.

It felt like every day, activities that had been deemed OK just twenty-four hours before would be banned, or businesses that were allowed to remain open would be forced to close. And while I totally understood the precautions, it sort of felt like there was an all-powerful lifeguard with a big hat and zinc-covered nose who kept wading into the ocean where the rest of us were trying to enjoy a little sun on our floaties to blow his whistle and scream on the bullhorn, "Nope! No, that's too far! Bring it back to shore!"

Amid all that craziness, I, like moms everywhere, was trying to figure out how to harmonize getting work done with educating and entertaining my kids, who are 17 months apart and will just as easily plot ways to kill each other as they will hug and snuggle together. Simultaneously, I had to come up with ways to feed my family creative renditions of tuna fish and keep my house from turning into a total pigsty. And I did more dishes and laundry than anyone has ever wanted to do in the history of the world, *ever*.

You could say I was in desperate need of some normalcy.

When your world is turned upside down, it's very tempting to give up. You start to wonder, would it really be so bad to walk around the house all day in jammies with a perpetually full glass of Chardonnay and just tell everyone else to "figure it out?" (Probably. Yes. It probably would be bad.)

Believe me, girlfriend, I had to dig deep to find a way to keep my world on its axis during that crisis, but I came out on the other side with tried-and-true ways for creating a sense of normalcy in a world full of chaos.

Here's what I suggest if you're ever faced with having to create a new "normal" when everything else feels like it's falling apart.

Make your bed.

Do it even if you don't leave the house and you're just going to get right back into it in a few hours. There is brain science that connects making your bed to having a great day. (Don't ask me for supporting sources! Just believe it!)

And it literally takes 45 seconds. Even if it's not something you would "normally" do, try it! If nothing else, seeing your pillows and blankets all perfectly coiffed will put a smile on your face.

Create a routine.

Humans crave routines. Knowing what to expect creates a sense of order and purpose, even when it feels like the rest of the world has lost their shit.

To be productive and effective when things are crazy, you cannot be in weekend mode every single day. Set an alarm. Go to bed on time. Eat proper meals. Plan out your week. Even if you don't have all that much to do, plan for and calendar all those things you always said you would do "when" you have time. Surely there's a junk drawer or linen closet that could use your attention?

You might (probably will) have to get creative and give yourself a ton of grace, but I promise you, having a routine will keep you sane.

Practice self-care, hard.

Your new routine most definitely must include time for self-care. Getting your mind right each day is the only way you will make it through a crisis without going straight-up nuts.

I do my self-care routine in the morning, before anyone else in my house is awake. I get peace and quiet and wide-open mental space to soak up some power and love before I start my day. That quiet time will look different for everyone, but whatever it looks like for you, give it to yourself. Meditate. Journal. Pray. Exercise. Be unapologetic about wanting to take care of yourself.

Living as your highest and best self means not trading away your beauty and strength, even when you're dealing with chaos. Your kiddos are watching everything you do. When things get tumultuous and uncertain, show them that the greatest thing they can do is love themselves by demonstrating that you love yourself.

Get dressed.

Everyone (including you) will take you more seriously if you aren't wearing pajamas all day.

Now, I'm not saying buttons and zippers are mandatory when life as you've known it has gone awry, but wear something you wouldn't be embarrassed to be caught in at the grocery store or while video chatting your mother-in-law or your boss.

Getting dressed is the lead domino that will knock down other power-inducing behavior, like brushing your teeth, washing your face, and holding your head up just a bit higher. Don't believe me? Step out of those sweatpants and try it for yourself, mama.

Oh, and definitely wear mascara.

Upgrade your five.

When your life is in turmoil, you cannot forget that you are the average of the five people you hang around the most. Be very intentional about who you listen to and who you lean on. The energy you allow into your space will make or break you.

Choose people who are contributing to the brightness and expansiveness of life. The podcasts you listen to and shows you watch can affect your mental health, for better or for worse. It matters who you allow to vent to you on the phone. Adjust who you're following on social media. Limit the news alerts you receive. And if you need to have a heart-to-heart with your family about supporting you in creating healthy energy in your home, do it.

Remember, even when life feels completely out of control, nothing good ever comes from making up a horror story in your head. Might as well just skip that whole exercise and focus on what you *can* control: who you listen to and what you believe.

Attention is everything. Surround yourself with like-minded people and put your attention on the ideal outcome.

Ride your new normal until the crisis dies out.

Because it *will* die out. Good is always on the horizon, girlfriend. This too, shall pass.

Chapter Thirty

BATTLING MOM BURNOUT

Before I had kids, I was convinced I'd be an awesome stay-at-home mom (or as all the cool kids say these days, a "SAHM").

"How hard could it be?" I asked myself when I got pregnant with my first child. After having spent almost seven years practicing commercial litigation for a highly respected international law firm, dueling it out in court, taking and defending depositions, wrangling demanding clients, playing law firm politics, and going tit-for-tat with opposing counsel for 60-plus hours a week, being a SAHM sounded like a total breeze.

Cue hysterical, uncontrollable laughter.

Boy, was I wrong.

Being a SAHM was the hardest job I've ever had. When my daughter was 9 months-old, just as I was beginning to feel like, *Yeah, baby, I got this!* I found out I was pregnant with my son. (I don't know who needs to read this, but you can indeed get pregnant while nursing, despite what your husband wants to believe.) In less time than it used to take me to resolve a big case, I had gone from a high-powered lawyer in pencil skirts and heels to an ex-

hausted mom of two under two who was, at any given moment, covered in
unidentified bodily fluids.

Two years after I had turned in my lawyer card to raise my family, I
realized I wasn't happy. Chasing one kid to ensure she didn't kill the other,
whilst simultaneously feeding, cleaning and entertaining both tiny humans,
and trying to be a homemaker and—oh, yeah—a wife had muted my identity. I had completely lost myself in motherhood. I had nothing that was mine
outside of being "Mommy" and "wife."

Although I was terrified people would think I was ungrateful, or worse,
that I didn't love my kids, I finally admitted out loud that I wanted—no,
needed—to go back to work.

I eased myself into it with a home-based business, and eventually started lawyering again in an office. My kids started school, and my brain started
firing in ways I hadn't realized I'd missed.

I felt accomplished and driven. I found myself again.

And then . . . March 2020 happened. Just like that—I was home with my
kids again and forced back into the role of SAHM. Only this time, I had the
responsibility and expectations of my career piled on top.

Each weekday morning, I would summon every ounce of willpower I
had from every part of my body to make distance learning fun and inter-
esting for my 6-year-old, who was, at any given moment, throwing himself
on the floor and whining about how boring I am. Meanwhile, I was also
fielding periodic interruptions from my 7-year-old, who would insist that
her math assignment "doesn't make any sense" (it always did make sense, by
the way, and that's coming from a math-illiterate lawyer) or announce to her
brother and I that she was not going to distract him from his school work . . .
thereby distracting him from his schoolwork with that very announcement.

Once that titillating fun was over and "school" was dismissed, I climbed
onto my creaky desk stool to log on to my laptop and do some lawyering.
Then at 5:30 PM, I would stuff my face with cheese, crackers, and Chardonnay in between chopping and sautéing dinner, or, if it was my husband's
turn to cook, I'd do the cheese-cracker-Chardonnay stuffing in front of an
HGTV "Home Town" marathon. Sometimes I'd fold laundry in the quiet
sanctuary of my bedroom as a treat to myself.

Swoonworthy, I know.

I quickly had to admit that I felt trapped. I had done both things before—worked at an intense and demanding job and stayed home to be my kiddos' teacher, a cook, a cleaning lady, and a fixer-of-all-situations—but never at the same time. And though my husband could very well be the most supportive man alive, the heavy lifting of nurturing our kids and keeping our home from looking like hoarders live in it naturally continued to fall to me, even if I had a conference call scheduled or a deadline to meet.

And even when we all began to feel some relief from the restrictions and kiddos went back to school and began resuming normal activities, I continued to experience an overwhelm and a burnout I couldn't shake. It felt as though working motherhood hadn't become any easier, it just became a different kind of hard.

Do you ever feel that way too? Rest assured, you're not alone. In fact, far from it, around 10 million working moms are struggling with burnout as we speak.

The good news is that you can absolutely regain your footing. Here's what worked for me during that most trying time and what I continue to rely on today.

Create an intentional plan.

The first person I opened up to about my struggle was my husband.

Having been down this road before as a SAHM, I knew better this time than to pretend I could handle it all myself. My strategy? Brutal and utter honesty.

I openly confessed my misery to him. I needed his help managing my kids' school days with my work schedule and the demands of our household.

So, we created an intentional plan. He agreed to completely handle the mornings, which includes getting the kids up, dressed, fed, and groomed, and he agreed to take them to school every day. I agreed to handle bedtime. Breaking it up that way made all the difference—for *all* of us. The energy I gained from taking a step away to do something just for me, even if it was work, spilled over into everything else I did. And, much to *everyone's* delight, my patience returned.

If your partner doesn't have the flexibility at work to help you, or if you're parenting solo, lean on someone outside your home if you can. From extended family to neighbors and friends, there are people in your life who want to help you. Don't martyr yourself or, even worse, believe the lie that you're a burden. Women love to help other women; most of us just need to be asked.

So ask.

Abandon the guilt.

It's so easy to buy into mom guilt when your kids are home with you, for whatever reason, and you maybe wish they weren't.

When I first began working from home after the pandemic normalized it, I found myself cycling through feelings of resentment when my children pulled me away from what I was working on, followed by intense guilt for not having the patience (or desire) to have them in my face for hours on end, and then back to resentment again.

Eventually, I realized the mom guilt didn't make me a better mom. You know what did? Acknowledging that being home with kids is hard and being unapologetic about taking designated time away to work on my own passions.

It's OK to have goals and dreams outside of your role as mom, and it's OK to want to work on them—even if it means your kids have to fend for themselves when they can't find their library books or socks. That doesn't make you "less" of a mom. It makes you human.

Let it all out.

As moms, we tend to put such intense pressure on ourselves to always keep it "together."

The truth is, it's OK to cry. Being upset with yourself for crying is kind of like berating yourself for having to pee. Obviously, there's a time and a place for everything. I don't walk around blubbering 24/7 without regard for my surroundings and I don't fall to pieces in front of my kids at every turn.

But I don't hold it in, either. Being a working mom today is hard. When I need to release the tears, I give myself that release. I vent freely to my best friends and my husband. I don't care what I sound like or how totally "untogether" I seem. I need to get it out—and so do you. It might look ugly for a hot minute, but you'll feel so much better afterwards. I guarantee it.

Remember that you're doing your very best. (Of course you are! You

didn't wake up today plotting all the ways you could be mediocre! *Come on.*)
Being a working mom isn't easy, but it means you get to teach your kids how
to handle adversity, how to show up for themselves, how to go after their
dreams and crush their goals, and how to get back up when they fall short.

Be nice to yourself. Give yourself grace as you navigate nurturing your
kids while nurturing your career.

You're an amazing mom. And you've totally got this.

Chapter Thirty-One

IT WON'T ALWAYS
WORK OUT

I wear my heart on my sleeve. I am fiercely loyal and I love deeply. I make friends quickly and I trust easily. Those traits allow me to have meaningful connections and incredible experiences.

They also, inevitably, set me up for some heartache and disappointment along the way.

Not too long ago, I experienced some of that heartache. Without getting into the gory details, I'll simply say it was the grownup equivalent of having your best classmate tell you she doesn't want to play with you anymore. Over text message. Complete with the old, "It's not you, it's me" song and dance.

Cue major eye roll.

But as silly as it sounds now, I was upset when it happened. OK, I'll be totally honest: I was crushed. I had thought this person was my friend and that we were going to create some amazing results for a joint endeavor we had been working on together. I felt blindsided when she told me (via text) that our partnership wasn't working for her and that she wanted to explore other options.

It was like being dumped. Used. Discarded.

So I let myself feel all the feels. I cried. I engaged in negative self-talk (*Do I suck? What's wrong with me? Am I not good enough?*). And after fully experiencing my emotions (except for the one where I wanted to go *Office Space* on a printer), I released it.

And, as I always strive to do after any life experience, I reflected on what this particular rejection taught me. Here's what I took away and what I'll help my kids take away when something doesn't work out for them.

Always listen to your intuition.

Or, put another way, trust your gut.

During our "friendship," I got little glimpses of this person that made me wonder if she was truly as genuine as she seemed, but I quickly brushed those thoughts off as unwarranted negativity, or paranoia, or another case of me "being in my head."

In hindsight, of course, it all fits together. Your intuition will never steer you wrong, girlfriend. There's an old saying: when people tell you who they are, listen.

In this case, listening to my intuition would have spared me the heartache. But I don't actually regret the way things went down. (More on that in a sec'.)

I am grateful, however, that I can see where my intuition was trying to point me, if for no other reason than it's comforting to know I can depend on that gift when it really matters.

Remember The Moana Principle.

I explained The Moana Principle in Chapter Twenty-Eight, but in case you're reading out of order, I'll quickly fill you in.

In the Disney movie *Moana*, there's a part when she's navigating the ocean on a raft, lost and alone, searching for Maui, a demi-god no one has seen in like, hundreds of years. She has absolutely no idea how she's going to find him, and in a moment of desperate faith, she calls on the ocean for help.

The ocean immediately throws her into a tumultuous storm while she hangs on for her life in terror. The next morning, she finds herself shipwrecked on an island, frazzled and disoriented, and seemingly no closer to finding Maui. Furious, she curses the ocean for toying with her, but in the next moment, who does she discover just happens to be stranded on that island too?

Maui.

The ocean delivered her *right to him.*

You see the metaphor, right? Sometimes the fastest way to get from where you are to where you need to be is through a complete shitstorm. This phenomenon is what I call The *Moana* Principle.

I'm grateful I was able to let that breakup experience reveal itself as a blessing in disguise. I quickly began to see how things aligned and came together for my benefit once the partnership ended, and I have complete trust and faith that I'll reach my goals even faster *because* it ended.

It didn't feel good when it was happening, but it's clear to me now that it needed to happen.

So next time life throws you a storm, try to see it for what it is: a shortcut to bigger and better. Don't resist it; don't curse it. Don't shut your eyes and wish it wasn't happening. Obviously, you need to experience it. After all, it's taking you exactly where you want to go.

Regret is a choice.

Remember earlier, when I said I don't regret the way this whole scenario went down?

Here's what I mean by that: had I avoided the heartache, I also would have missed out on the fun.

I had some great times with this person while it lasted and learned strategies and skills I probably would not have learned otherwise, if she and I hadn't been pushing toward a goal together. I don't regret that for one second.

Realize that regret is a choice. And when we choose regret instead of choosing to see the value that exists in every experience, we allow ourselves to be robbed.

I don't know about you, but I refuse to give my time and energy away by choosing regret. More importantly, I'm teaching my kids about that choice. I'm showing them exactly what it looks like—ugly tears and all—to move on after feeling sad and rejected and how to turn tough experiences into powerful life lessons.

We are forged in the fire, my friend. Sometimes, it's just not supposed to work out. But disappointment and heartache only make us stronger, and you know what? They make us better mamas too.

Chapter Thirty-Two

NOT EVERYONE IS GONNA
THINK YOU'RE AWESOME

My love language is "words of affirmation," which I always thought was adorable until I realized that I'm sort of saying I need other people to tell me how awesome I am to feel worthy or loved.

Wait. That doesn't sound powerful . . .

But it has played out that way in real life, with me craving, more than I'd like to admit, affirmation and praise as a way to feel good enough.

Good enough as a lawyer. Good enough as a podcaster. Good enough as an author and a business owner. Good enough as a mom.

Do you ever go there too?

Not too long ago, someone ranked me at the bottom of their list. Literally, it was a written list. In my mind, they were saying, "We don't care how hard you've been working. We still think you are the least capable member of this group." And for a solid hour, I acted like what they thought actually mattered. I felt like I *needed* their belief in me.

That was stupid.

But it was also a great lesson. Because the truth is that not everyone is going to believe in me. Not everyone is going to think I'm awesome.

They're wrong, though.

I believe in me. And that's enough. That belief is what keeps me going in every single one of my personal and professional endeavors and helps me show up again and again to make an impact on working mamas.

Same goes for you, girlfriend. There will always be people in your life who don't think you're awesome, whether it's a co-worker, another mom, a teammate, or even a member of your own family.

But what other people think of you or say about you or say to you doesn't change who you are. And it never can.

So be who you are. Because you're amazing.

Chapter Thirty-Three

"MOTHER" BELONGS ON YOUR RESUME

I used to think "working" and "mother" did not belong in the same sentence.

That was the main reason I quit my job after giving birth to my daughter. I could see what I was up against. There's no question that the professional world hasn't always been super mom-friendly. We face a very real cultural bias in the workplace that's pretty much impossible to ignore.

But now that I'm a little wiser, I seriously don't understand why.

Being a mom is a professional asset. Truly. Motherhood trains a woman, in an almost unforgiving, bootcamp-ish way, how to be a leader.

Yet if we're being honest with ourselves, we sometimes shy away from embracing that notion. Isn't your knee-jerk reaction to apologize when one of your kiddos busts in on a Zoom meeting? Haven't you ever worried colleagues will view you as inflexible if you need to schedule calls around feedings or naptime or felt guilty for logging off early to take kids to their after-school activities?

Trust me, I know the desire to be the consummate professional at all times is real.

Before I became a mom, I was a lawyer practicing commercial litigation for a prestigious, international law firm. (Translation: I got paid to go to court on behalf of big companies and fight about money all day long.) I fully understand what it's like to shoulder the pressure to constantly be "on."

And then I had kids. After a two-year stint as a stay-at-home mom that ended when I finally admitted to myself that I would never be the wife or mother I wanted to be if I didn't have something that was just mine, I decided to go back to work.

But this time, I had an entirely different perspective. Don't get me wrong—I definitely worried at first about having to explain to employers the gap on my resume.

I'm not marketable anymore. My skills aren't sharp. I've been out of the game for too long.

And then I remembered my training. I'm the CEO of my entire household, ensuring that all humans within it remain healthy, fed, bathed, clothed, loved, educated, entertained, and active each day. I'm responsible for managing schedules, deadlines, *and* attitudes. There have been times I've had to do all that on less than three hours of sleep, with dirty hair and teeth and spit-up on my shirt. And I do it all for a whopping annual salary of zero dollars.

That truth bomb helped me realize I am extremely valuable in the workplace—not despite being a mother, but *because* I am.

So I'm owning it. Here's why I'm putting "Mother" on my resume (and why you should too).

Being a mom means knowing how to juggle important tasks.

Motherhood is a constant act of juggling (not to be confused with "multitasking," which is the false premise that we can do two things at once).

As moms, we're required to alternate giving our full attention to different but equally important areas of our lives daily, like nurturing our marriages, taking care of our minds and bodies, keeping our houses (somewhat) clean, and our laundry (sort of) done—not to mention keeping our kids alive.

This innate ability translates easily to the professional world, where, as a bonus, the environment is relatively quiet and presumably no one ever threatens to pee on the floor. Yes, I can prepare that motion to dismiss and take on research about The Consumer Protection Act and find time for document review, and no, I'm not gonna freak out about it.

In other words, when it comes to managing more than one project at work, we moms can say with absolute certainty, "That won't be a problem. Bring it."

No one diffuses conflict like a mama.

Keeping our kids from killing each other and deciding what's "fair" is a routine part of being a mother.

Have you ever encountered humans who argue more heatedly than siblings over an iPad or what to watch on *PBS Kids?* I don't know about you, but I've been refereeing fights since the moment my oldest could say, "Mine!"

At work, we naturally act as the voice of reason when stress levels are running high. We can settle disputes between co-workers. We know how to calm irate clients. Being the arbiter of squabbles between our kids has given us a highly valuable skill set—and we sharpen it. Every. Single. Day.

We think on our feet.

I've never met a boss who doesn't love an employee who can quickly devise Plan B when Plan A goes sideways. Being able to think quickly on your feet is vital during client proposals, courtroom presentations, and product launches alike, and it's a prowess all moms employ regularly.

Having kids means dealing with unpredictability. We know better than anyone that things will not always go according to plan. (Seriously, you only have to lose electricity or the internet once to become a pro at selling "what we're gonna do instead.") Whipping a contingency plan out of our back pockets when things go awry comes naturally to most moms.

Moms are super prepared.

Perhaps because we often suspect our well-laid plans will be foiled, us mothers automatically prepare for any and all "just in case" scenarios. (After the first time your kid puked in the backseat of your car, you now remember ginger ale and barf bags on every trip, am I right?) That's why our purses are so heavy, and our cars are stocked for an apocalypse.

It's also why we're the women people want on their teams. We think of things like loading a back-up copy of the PowerPoint presentation to Google Drive in the event something goes wrong with the laptop at the client meeting. We bring extra case law to our hearings just in case the judge goes down a rabbit hole and asks a random question. And, of course, we always have a snack handy.

Clearly, "Mother" has earned a spot on all of our resumes.

We should be highlighting the fact that we're moms, not glossing over it. It's time to be unapologetic about the unique skills motherhood has given us. Let's celebrate that bringing life into this world enhances our ability to go after our professional goals and dreams and gives us the most beautiful, messy, exhausting, revered position we'll ever have the glory of holding.

Chapter Thirty-Four

YOU CAN FIND GOLD IN
THE UNLIKELIEST PLACES

Years ago, I had a foray in direct sales. My decision to dive into the direct selling world was born from a lack of fulfillment, boredom, and a smidge of desperation.

Wait. That sounds dramatic. Let me back up.

See, before I became a mom, I was a lawyer practicing commercial litigation for a prestigious, international law firm.

Suffice it to say, I didn't love my job, despite being compensated well, having a strong sense of independence, and, admittedly, feeling kind of important when I went to court and judges listened to me when I talked. At the end of the day, it was a grind and a half.

So when I became pregnant with my daughter, I hatched a diabolical plan with my husband whereby I would pay down as much of my law school debt as possible before giving birth, and once our daughter was born, I'd quit to be a stay-at-home mom.

Our plan went swimmingly. We paid down my student loans, I gave birth to a beautiful baby girl, took my full twelve weeks' maternity leave, and, when I returned to the office, promptly gave my notice. I bid farewell to Big Law like, *"Peace out, homies!"* and stepped into my new role as CEO of Casa Oden without looking back.

But fast forward two years, and I had gone from a high-powered lawyer in pencil skirts and heels to an exhausted mom of two under 2 who was fairly consistently covered in bodily fluids that were not her own. After a lot of denial, I finally admitted out loud that I wasn't happy.

The truth was I had completely lost myself in motherhood.

I had nothing that was mine outside of being "Mommy" and "wife." I knew to find myself again, I needed something just for *me*.

The thought of going back to Big Law gave me hives though, so I decided to start a direct sales business from home instead. I began my career with an organic food company and then moved on to one of the largest cosmetic and skin care companies in the world. At both places I saw tremendous success, earning all-expenses-paid vacations for me and my husband at the first company and a free car at the second.

Now, let me stop right here and acknowledge the elephant in the room.

I know direct sales gets a bad rap in the media. And as someone who's actually walked the walk as a direct seller, I can sort of understand where some of that negative press comes from. But I also know being in direct sales can add immense value to your life. Golden nuggets, if you will.

Here's what I learned and continue to use daily in my mom life, and you can too.

Always ask for what you want.

When your job is to sell products, book parties, and recruit new team members, you have to do a lot of asking. Like, a lot a lot. Over the years I realized asking for what you want is a skill that applies to all areas of your life.

"Do you have any more sizes in the back?"

"Can I get that without cilantro and add tomatoes and cucumbers?"

"Will you please donate to my kids' school fundraiser?"

"Will you pay me $100 per published article instead of $75?"

What's the worst that can happen? They say no? OK, fine. Let's indulge this terrifying what-if scenario. They say no. And . . . are you any worse off than if you hadn't asked?

Nope.

But what if they say yes?

To paraphrase the Bible, you have not because you ask not. Ask for what you want, girlfriend.

Be nice to strangers for no reason at all.

When I was a sales director for the cosmetics and skincare company, one of the ways I was taught to find new hostesses and team members was to genuinely compliment random strangers wherever I went and then invite them to the latest event I had on the books. We called it "warm chatting," and although it made me cringe, it also led to me meeting some amazing women with whom I'm still friends to this day.

After I stepped down from my leadership role with that company to start Your Ideal Mom Life®, I found myself continuing to warm chat, without the pitch.

"Your eyelashes are amazing."

"You have gorgeous skin."

"I love your nail color."

And you know what? I discovered that it feels good to hand out compliments. Try it. At worst, some rando at Target you'll never see again thinks you're nuts.

At best, you make another woman's day.

Put yourself out there.

Direct sales ain't nothin' if not a repeated series of putting yourself out there. Is it possible people will make fun of you? Yep. Might they reject your offer? You betcha. Is it scary? Uh, *yeah.*

But the more you put yourself out there, the closer you get to your goal. And more importantly—the more you grow.

Listen, girlfriend. You think Oprah became *Oprah* by playing it small? Do you think Amazon would exist if Jeff Bezos hadn't put it all on the line and fought to make a dream born in his garage a reality, despite all his critics? Would you and I even be friends if I hadn't decided to put my soul on paper and publish this book?

Remember that your kids are watching you. When they see you do hard things, they learn that they can do hard things, too. They grow from watching you stretch yourself and play full out. They emulate how you deal with adversity and disappointment and make the connection when they see you go after your goals and achieve big things.

And they notice when you don't. They see all the times you choose to settle instead. So get out there, mama.

Try out for the ladies doubles league at the tennis center.

Apply for the Executive Board of the PTA.

Ask for the promotion.

Start your own company.

Run for office.

Be the girl who puts herself out there and just goes for it.

Be very intentional with your time.

You and I both know being a mom involves a beastly time-management struggle.

Keeping the small humans in your house fed, bathed, educated, active, and entertained on a daily basis is no joke. And of course, that's on top of brushing your own teeth and hair, eating, sleeping, exercising, and nurturing your relationship with your spouse. Add a home-based business to the mix and things can get ugly, *fast.*

Being your own boss requires a set of habits most of us simply didn't pick up in our early years, like being intentional with the 24 hours we have each day. Having a direct sales business brutally exposed my deficiencies in this area and led to me living in survival mode for several years.

But eventually, through lots of trial and improvement, I figured it out.

Today, I'm a time-management ninja. And I can tell you with absolute certainty that doing a mental dump, prioritizing, and time blocking are vital not only to running a business but to creating a mom life you love. No doubt, there is a very real relationship between feeling confident and powerful in your mom life and deliberately planning out your week in advance.

Remember: you are the center of your household. When you become intentional with your time, you stop feeling overwhelmed and spread thin and start experiencing more patience and joy, and that will spill over into everything you do. Everything.

I'm telling you, friend, this stuff is legit.

Don't make up stories in your head about why other people do the things they do.

During my direct sales career, I reached out to a lot of people, met a ton more, and planted a lot of seeds. And let me tell you: not all of those seeds sprouted. That means I sent, like, a gazillion texts and emails that went unanswered and made plenty of phone calls that were never returned.

At first, the temptation to invent a story in my head about why I didn't hear back was almost irresistible.

They don't like me.

Maybe she thinks I'm pushy and annoying.

She wants to say no but doesn't know how to tell me.

And while, sure, some of those stories were undoubtedly true, the reality was that it usually wasn't any of those things. In fact, most of the time it had absolutely nothing to do with me or my business.

Eventually, I realized I needed to give people grace and stop making everything about me.

Most people are completely absorbed in their own stuff. They're not plotting all the ways they can be intentionally rude or unresponsive. No one wakes up in the morning and asks herself, "How can I be a jerk today?"

So when people don't respond to your text messages or call you back, if they ignore your emails, when they unfriend or unfollow you—don't let yourself think for one second that you *actually* know why.

In most cases, it ain't got nothin' to do with you. Maybe you reached out at the precise moment her kid barfed in the car, and therefore, responding to you is (obviously) not a priority. Perhaps her baby got a hold of her phone and unfriended all of her friends on social media. Maybe her email got hacked, and she deleted her account.

Give people the benefit of the doubt and don't make it about you.

So. Freeing.

I know direct sales isn't for everyone, and that's a beautiful thing. You're shining in your unique gifts and talents, and the world needs that. In the end, direct sales wasn't my forever career either, but I'm glad I had the experience. Aren't you? It led me to creating Your Ideal Mom Life® and writing this book—a calling I would never have otherwise discovered.

Wherever you are on your journey, keep shining, girlfriend. Don't underestimate where your path is leading you. And don't forget to share all the beautiful nuggets you pick up along the way.

Chapter Thirty-Five

RAISING BRAVE KIDS

I do affirmations with my kids.

It dawned on me one day when they were really little that kids are mean. And some day, in the distant future, those mean kids might tell my adorable, sweet, innocent little babies that they're dumb. Or weird. Or bad at sports. You know—the stuff You-Can't Monsters are made of. And in that moment of realization, I felt myself getting offended and mad. I was like, *"Aw, heck no!"* (I'm not the only woman who goes mama bear over situations that haven't happened yet, am I?)

The imaginary bullying got me thinking . . . how can I prepare them for the inevitable trials of youth and adolescence, like the mean girls and the merciless boy hazing? How do I prepare them for the stuff beyond all that, like the scariness of choices and trying something new and putting yourself out there?

I'm not sure any mom can fully prepare her kids for rejection and failure and, you know . . . high school. But a girl can try.

I settled on affirmations.

And so, since they were little I have told them every day, "You are smart, kind, and important. You can do hard things. You don't give up easily." As they got bigger, we added a few to the list, like "I try new things" (that one was very useful for when we were introducing new foods) and, "I say please and thank you" (very effective for instilling manners). We always end with, "You're brave. You're powerful."

Now that my kids are old enough to have real conversations and strong opinions, I don't have to say the affirmations to them anymore. Instead, I say, "Tell me who you are." And they say the affirmations to me. Sometimes they say them begrudgingly, with a little eye roll, but by the time they get to the end of the list, I always get a robust and authentic, *"I'm POWERFUL!"*

It's like, totally adorable. And tear-jerking. And it makes my heart burst with pride.

Knowing who you are is a gift no one can ever take away from you. When my kids are afraid to try, I want them to draw courage by remembering who they are. I want them to push through no matter how afraid they are to fail, because even when failure is a very real possibility, they'll always be kind, smart, and important.

And just in case that's not enough, I show them. Every day, I show them what courage looks like by admitting to them when I'm afraid to do something, and then *I do it anyway.* I jump into the cold pool. I get on the roller-coaster. I publish the book.

Raising brave kids starts with being brave ourselves.

When you're scared, be scared. And then remember who you are. You are kind. You are smart. You are important. Trust yourself. Show your kids what being brave looks like and do the thing anyway.

Chapter Thirty-Six

PERFECT, SCHMERFECT

At my daughter's end-of-year celebration when she was in first grade, her teacher took a few moments to speak to each student individually in front of the crowd.

The audience consisted of my daughter's classmates and the parents and grandparents who had gathered in her classroom to celebrate. My husband and I stood among them, exchanging polite and knowing smiles with the other parents as we collectively watched our big kids getting even bigger, moving on from first grade up to second.

When it was my daughter's turn, the teacher called her up out of her seat. She wrapped her arms around my little goose and praised her for being such a hard worker and for always doing her very best. Then she pulled back from her so she could look into my daughter's wide green eyes and said, "I just want you to know, Emma, that you're amazing the way you are. You don't have to be perfect."

I flinched imperceptibly. Tears stung my eyes, and I knew in that moment she was speaking to me, to that part of me I passed down to Emma, the same part I inherited from my own mother.

I nodded firmly in agreement, although Emma couldn't see me from where her beautiful face was buried again in her teacher's dress. I wanted to put my hands on her shoulders and squeeze them to underline what her teacher had said.

You don't have to be *perfect*.

I want her to believe the words. I want her to understand them. I want her to give herself the full experience of her life, to revel in the freedom of releasing the results. "It's OK to make mistakes," I wanted to call to her from across the room.

And it is. It is OK.

As a woman who has struggled heartily with perfectionism and who has always been brutally hard on herself, I endeavor now as a mother to teach my children this lesson. Mistakes are simply evidence you are trying. If you aren't making mistakes, you aren't trying *hard enough*. Everything you create, especially your mistakes, is a gift. Your mistakes are an opportunity to grow, to make yourself better. It is only from the ash that the phoenix rises.

Remember that today, girlfriend. You are already amazing. You don't have to be perfect.

Chapter Thirty-Seven

HOW TO CHOOSE GREATNESS
WHEN YOU FEEL LIKE YOU SUCK

I met Gigi Fernandez once.

You know—the tennis legend? She's won 17 Grand Slams in doubles. To give you context, Wimbledon, which you've certainly heard of, is a Grand Slam and she's won it *four times.* And even if you're not a tennis follower, surely you've heard of the Olympics? Well, she's won the Gold medal in doubles for the United States *twice,* back-to-back.

In other words, she's ah-*mazing* at doubles.

As I may have mentioned once or twice, I love tennis. Like, a lot. I love talking about it, reading about it, playing it. I even love watching other people play it, and not just professionals. Shawn always chuckles when he catches me staring at random strangers hitting a ball back and forth on courts along our favorite bike path in Sanibel Island. "You're a student of the game," he says.

Probably an understatement, but yes, I am. So when I found out one day that Gigi was offering a tennis camp just three hours from my home, I was like, *Of course I'm doing that.* Now, even if you never plan to pick up a tennis racquet as long as you live, keep reading. Tennis camp, as it turns out, is full of life lessons.

It was taught both on and off the court. During some of the on-court moments, I started to realize that I kind of sucked. Objectively, I was the least-skilled player of the eight of us who were there. Although I took some solace in the fact I was also the youngest by far, I had a few moments where I felt like standing on the sidelines and just watching.

But I knew if I surrendered to that feeling, the camp would be a waste. I had gone there to learn from a legend, after all, and stewing on just how *much* I had to learn was not going to help me.

It was through my experience with Gigi Fernandez that I learned greatness is a choice. Being far from where you want to be doesn't mean you aren't great at what you do. It seems to me that perhaps no one understands this better than she does. Here's what I learned from Gigi about how to choose greatness (even when you feel like you suck), in both tennis and in life.

Act like you're having fun, even if you're not.

During one of our "classroom" moments at camp, Gigi recounted a time early in her career at the U.S. Open when she was *not* having fun.

In fact, she had already made up her mind that the tournament was going to be her last Grand Slam. She was quitting tennis as soon as it was over and heading back to Puerto Rico to "get married and have babies." Before she carried out this diabolical plan, however, she had the sense to employ the advice of a brilliant sports psychologist with whom she'd just begun working.

"Act like you're having fun," he'd told her. "Even if you're not."

Gigi relayed that, at first, she found this advice absurd. How do you act like you're having fun when you're not? But she tried it, albeit begrudgingly at first. After each match she won in the tournament, he would ask her, "Are you having fun?"

"No, I'm not having fun!" she would respond. "I'm stressed!"

But wouldn't you know it? As she continued to pretend she was having fun, she continued to win her matches. And at the very end, she'd won the whole damn tournament.

By then, of course, she was having a blast.

I love that story because it's so relatable to our everyday lives. Where in your life could you benefit from acting like you're having fun, even if you're not? When you're losing the match? When your kids are making you nuts? When the weight-loss journey is grueling and difficult? When the obstacles between you and your dreams keep popping up like land mines?

As much as you want to throw yourself on the ground and kick and scream (or is that just me?), try imagining, instead, how you would behave if you were having fun. And to be clear, I'm not saying you shouldn't allow yourself to experience anger and frustration. On the contrary, you absolutely *should* because those creations will find their way out one way or another, and you *know* it will be at the most embarrassing or inconvenient time. Haven't you ever burst into tears at work or at the grocery store? (Or again, is that just me?)

What I am saying is, from a place of awareness of your feelings, intentionally shift and behave *as if* you're having fun.

You'll feel like a big phony at first. You may even feel ridiculous. You definitely won't feel like you're having fun. Until suddenly, you *do*. And that, my friend, is where the magic happens. That one decision holds so much power. How much easier do you think it is to play full-out, to referee arguments between your kids, to keep going even when the scale is telling you a different story—when you're having fun?

Uh, you probably don't need to guess. It's a lot easier.

But it goes beyond that. Where would we all be if Gigi hadn't employed this advice all those years ago? What if she had indeed quit tennis? It's profound to think of all the people she would never have inspired, the records she would never have set, the lives she would never have touched.

That same thought is true for you too. What if you're holding yourself back from your destiny? What if harnessing your power is on the other side of making that simple switch to acting like you're having fun, even when you're not?

You cannot forget, even in those hard moments, that you are destined for greatness. Rise up and claim it, mama.

Talk to yourself.

Wahoo! Got that one down.

In all seriousness, Gigi means talk to yourself the way you would talk to someone you love. Encourage yourself. Pump yourself up.

This tip is particularly effective whenever you're required to perform, whether it's during a tennis match, presenting at a board meeting, or throwing a big dinner party. Ideally, you would talk to yourself in your head and not out loud if you're amongst strangers, but if you need to take a mutter under your breath, I say, go for it. When I'm at the gym, I encourage myself loudly. I'm pretty sure the people nearby can hear me, but I don't care. How else am I supposed to do a pull-up?

My go-to is, "You got this." Sometimes I'll throw in a, "Yes you can," which is in direct response to the voice in my head that just said, "I can't do this." Often, I'll add a physical element to my self-talk too. I'll give myself a double thump over the heart, gangsta style, or I'll lightly slap the outside of my thigh, like I'm trying to giddyup a horse. Gigi tells herself, "You can do it."

And guess what, girlfriend? YOU. CAN.

The goal should not be to win.

I know this seems counterintuitive. Isn't that everyone's ultimate goal: to win?

Historically, it certainly has been mine. But after being at camp with Gigi, it seems to me that losing your death grip on the win is how you crush a huge, terrifying goal—like starting a new business, leaving a toxic marriage, winning Wimbledon, whatever—without becoming paralyzed by the weight of its importance. As Gigi explains, winning is simply the culmination of everything you did leading up to that moment.

It's the result of consistent effort, day in and day out. Winning happens at the end.

In other words? "Detach from the outcome," she says. Commit to the process. Focus on being excellent at the elements that comprise the win. In tennis, that might mean moving your feet, watching the ball, transferring your weight forward, or keeping your tossing arm up on your serve. In life, it could mean waking up early to dedicate the first 30 minutes of every day to honing your craft, devising that business plan, or sweating your face off during another intense training session. Releasing the result and committing to the process without fail, even when no one is watching, is how you *get* the win.

So don't be afraid of your giant dreams. After all, when the goal is not to win, there's no need to feel overwhelmed. Take it one point at a time. When you do that often enough, with consistency, the win is inevitable.

You already have it.

The greatest lesson I learned from Gigi was completely unspoken.

Quite simply, she showed me what I'm capable of. You would be amazed by what you can do when you believe you cannot fail. I experienced this phenomenon in the final minutes of the camp when I created the tennis experience of a lifetime and (squeal!) got to play doubles *with Gigi Fernandez*. With Gigi as my partner, I knew we could not lose. I simply knew it as a fact, the way I know my eyes are brown and the sky is blue.

From that place of knowledge and belief, I accessed a power within me that I can honestly say I've only tapped into a handful of times. I went for it on my serve. I was aggressive with my ground strokes. I emphatically won us a point with a *backhand* volley (and mind you, I almost always hit backhand volleys into the neighboring court). In other words, because I believed we would dominate, I *behaved* like a dominator. And here's the kicker: *it worked.*

Where in your life could this be true for you? Where do you find yourself waiting for a "Gigi" to step onto the court alongside you before you'll access the power you *already* have? What if, instead, you just decided to believe in yourself the way I did that one time at tennis camp? Do you think you could do hard things? Tackle big, hairy, audacious goals?

Oh yeah, girlfriend. And the results? They'll. Be. Amazing.

So what are you waiting for? Start choosing greatness.
And by the way, you don't suck.

Chapter Thirty-Eight

FOUR BOOKS EVERY MOM SHOULD READ

I've always been a major bookworm. Growing up, I wasn't that girl who was into cheerleading or dance. I didn't play a sport.

I read. A lot.

The Babysitters Club series, thrillers by Christopher Pike and R.L. Stine, coming-of-age novels by Judy Blume, and every *single* literary work based on Elizabeth and Jessica Wakefield—from Sweet Valley Twins to Sweet Valley High to Sweet Valley University and all the Sweet Valley Saga stories—you name it, I read it. I had my nose in a book for most of my adolescence.

As a grown up, I haven't made as much time for fiction as I did as a tween, although I am a sucker for anything written by Jennifer Weiner, Taylor Jenkins Reid, or Emily Henry and have fallen hard for the *Outlander* series by Diana Gabaldon—and will finish them, however long it takes me! Instead, I've found myself devouring personal development books on Audible. (By the way, if you've never tried Audible, you must. You can legit consume a book and drive. It's the coolest thing ever.)

These four books are totes worth the read (or listen, as the case may be) and have given me some of my most powerful tools for creating a mom life I love. And I truly believe every mother should read them because being a mom is the most intense form of leadership you'll ever know. So why not level up?

The One Thing, by Gary Keller and Jay Papasan

I find myself returning to the principles of this book over and over again as I navigate the challenges of being a working mother who is also running a small business.

The ONE Thing taught me everything I know about productivity and prioritizing. I used to believe all things matter equally. They don't. *The ONE Thing* shows you how to focus so that, in going after your big, hairy, audacious goals, you can identify the one thing you can do to make everything else easier or unnecessary.

I know, I know. What does that mean, exactly?

Think of the steps toward achieving any goal as a row of evenly spaced dominoes. The easiest way to knock them all down is simply to knock over the first one, right? *The ONE Thing* explains that this principle applies to the achievement of any extraordinary result in life or business and gives you the tools to identify the lead dominoes in your own life.

Throughout most of my life, I've tended to overcomplicate things. Learning how to make things simpler in both my business and my mom life has been incredibly valuable.

You Are a Badass, by Jen Sincero

The mind is an incredibly powerful thing. As a recovering perfectionist, I have spent a lot of time in my head, painstakingly over-analyzing and worrying.

Through the power of self-discovery, I've learned how to command my thoughts and attention to create what I want to experience. *You Are a Badass* reinforces many of those principles and helps me remember that the universe is friendly and wants me to have my heart's deepest desires. I'm the only thing standing in my way.

I'd venture to say the same is true for you, my friend.

The Power of Habit, by Charles Duhigg

F.M. Alexander once said, "People don't decide their futures. They decide their habits, and their habits decide their futures." It's a powerful thought, and one I happen to agree with entirely after reading *The Power of Habit.*

A habit, according to Merriam-Webster, is "an acquired mode of behavior that has become nearly or completely involuntary."

Did you read that? *Involuntary.* In other words, once something becomes a habit, it requires *zero willpower or effort* on your part.

Imagine how much you could achieve if you intentionally created habits that serve you?

The Power of Habit explains the "habit loop," which enables you to understand how habits are formed and how they can be broken. Coupled with *The ONE Thing,* I've learned how to turn my lead dominoes into habits.

Life changing, mama. Life. Changing.

The 10x Rule, by Grant Cardone

This book is all about how to achieve big goals by taking massive action that most people simply will not take.

While I'll state openly that I don't agree with *everything* Mr. Cardone says in this book, one of the "aha!" moments I took from it is not to be afraid of problems. Every time you hit a new level of success, you will be presented with a new set of problems, guaranteed.

But that's a good thing. It means you're growing. If you lose 100 pounds and have to buy an entirely new wardrobe, that's a problem that needs to be solved, right? But it's a problem that came as a result of you achieving your goal and is, therefore, something to be welcomed.

This principle reminds me of a quote my business coach and mentor, Susie Moore, often repeats: "Overwhelm is a stress response to a lot of things going right." I'll take that kind of overwhelm any day.

Fair warning: Mr. Cardone is definitely an "in your face" kind of guy. In the Audible version of his book, which he narrates himself, he shares that he was going to call Chapter 6, "Don't Be a Little Bitch," but in an effort not to offend anyone, instead titled it, "Assume Control for Everything." The main idea is that "crybabies, whiners, and victims just don't do well at attracting or creating success."

Personally, I *love* that. I enjoy being held accountable.

There's something very empowering about realizing *you* create what you experience—good and bad. And the simplicity is kind of beautiful: there's really only one person to "blame" when things don't go right, and she's staring back at me when I look in a mirror.

While it can be hard to swallow when what you create is not so ideal, it's also pretty wild to realize you create the good stuff too. I love being reminded to step into my God-given power to create what I want to experience. It's very cool stuff.

So there you have it! The four books that changed my life. Go get to reading, mama. And if you still believe you "don't have time" to sit down with a book, then just use Audible while you drive, work out, or do laundry .

Leaders are readers, and you, my friend, are one of the most powerful leaders in the world: a mother. Give yourself the gift of personal growth. You deserve it.

Chapter Thirty-Nine

YOU CAN DO HARD THINGS

I hate running.

It's always seemed so pointless to me. I mean, why run just to run, without a destination or an identified purpose? Unless someone is chasing you, it just seems unnecessarily strenuous.

But you can't grow by staying inside your comfort zone. I understand that undeniable truth, and when an opportunity arises, I find myself jumping into experiences that I know will stretch me beyond my known limits. You don't know what you don't know, as the saying goes.

I say, *you don't know what you don't know until you do.* And you can only know what's unknown by trying new things, right?

So that's why, even though I hate to run and even though I was straight-up terrified of the many—*many*—pull-ups, pushups, burpees, and squats I knew awaited me, I begrudgingly signed up for an insane fitness challenge that I had once scoffed at as being inhumane and agreed to forego wine and coffee (among many of life's other delights) for four weeks in the name of fitness. The program consisted of a strict Paleo diet that made me wince at first glance (*"What do you mean, no hummus?!"*) and a workout regimen that had me doing handstand pushups on Saturdays. (To answer your question, yes, I modified them.) Any time I had a serving of alcohol, I would have to run a mile. And did I mention that the four weeks encompassed Mother's Day, the most glorious of all days to eat brunch?

Yet I dove in anyway, jitterbugs be damned. My goal was not to lose weight or inches, although I lost plenty of both. It wasn't even to win. It was just to finish the challenge and give it my all so that I would *know*: can I do it?

As it turns out, yes, I can! And as growth opportunities often do, this journey changed my life.

Not only did I make a life-long friend in the partner to whom I was randomly assigned, I became physically stronger, mentally tougher, grittier, and more resilient than I believed was possible. I can, like, totally do a real pushup now. Running ain't no thing anymore. I kicked caffeine for good. I am now a Paleo ninja. Oh, and my partner and I came in first place at the end of the four weeks, which was pretty cool too.

The moral?

Crushing a goal is dirty, hard work.

It's sweaty and gross. It's painful and challenging and, in my case, can bring you to your knees gasping for air or leave you face down on a trodden gym floor trying not to cry as you force yourself up for burpee number 15 of 22.

But it's also where you learn the nooks and crannies of who you are and who you're becoming. It's where the magic happens.

What's your "insane fitness challenge?" You know—that thing in the periphery that you think you could never do but would secretly love to give a shot? Do you want to publish a book? Open a bakery? Start a home-based business? Lose 25 pounds?

And who might you be at the end of that journey? Might you be stronger and more resilient? More willing to give yourself experiences that fortify your self-belief?

We all know what quitting feels like. Challenge yourself to taste what it would be like to try something new, finish what you start, and finish strong.

Chapter Forty

GIVE YOURSELF CREDIT FOR
HOW FAR YOU'VE COME

People say life begins at forty.

I think they say that to comfort themselves about getting older because people also say that life begins at fifty and then at sixty, but alas, I digress.

No matter how old you are today, give yourself credit for how far you've come. Imagine what bits of wisdom you would impart to your 25-year-old self if you could sit down and enjoy a glass of Chardonnay together.

For me, I think it would go something like this.

You're gonna fall on your face.

A lot. Don't resist it. Don't berate yourself for not getting it "right." *Your most brilliant moments will be born from those so-called failures.* You'll end up marrying the love of your life—after you marry the wrong guy first. You'll ditch that career you toiled away in school for, and that everyone else thought made you so successful, but that you secretly hated.

And you'll make friends who are true.

You'll discover you have a gift you can parlay into a career you absolutely love. You'll find your purpose. You'll find yourself.

Becoming a mom is the hardest thing you'll ever do.

Like, ever.

You'll start worrying the minute you know you're carrying that baby and you will never, ever stop. Not when you make it to 12 weeks. Not when the nuchal translucency screening comes back normal. Not when she's born and she's perfect and beautiful. Not even now, when she's 10 years old and a totally legit human with opinions and goals.

Oh, and nursing and sleep training are going to kick your ass. You are going to cry a *lot.* And then you're gonna have another baby 17 months later and do it all over again. (I know, girlfriend. *I know.*)

But you know what else? You're going to discover how precious life is. You're going to learn how to give grace to others and to yourself. You're going to understand from a place deep within your soul that a mother's love for her children is infinite.

And you're going to realize you've been kind of bratty to your own mom for a few decades, so be nicer to her, OK?

Try new things.

Listen, girlfriend. You've got mad skills.

Did you know you can pick up a sport as an adult and actually become good at it? Well, you can! And you will. (Tennis, anyone?) You're also going to start working out like a beast when you discover—almost unwittingly —that CrossFit is not just for crazy people. It's also for ordinary, mild-mannered, sleep-deprived moms who wanna lose some baby weight. And who woulda thunk it? You're going to enjoy it so much that working out is going to become a habit.

You're also going to become a scrapbooker. And a home cook. And a podcaster. And a woman who can rock fake eyelashes. And all of it will feel a little scary and uncomfortable at first, but you're gonna keep getting uncomfortable and trying new things.

In fact, you're going to stretch yourself beyond your comfort zone over and over again because you'll figure out that *growth is impossible inside your comfort zone.* The magic happens out "there," in the unknown.

Embrace it. It's really fun out there.

You'll discover what you love.

As a byproduct of trying new things, you'll learn what it's like to truly enjoy life and how to give yourself what you deserve.

You'll become *unapologetic about choosing joy.* You'll learn how to be still, how to allow, how to receive.

You'll learn to love yourself and who you're becoming.

You're gonna be OK, girlfriend.

Everything is going to happen exactly the way it's supposed to because the nonnegotiable truth is that you create what you experience.

You are powerful beyond measure. Everything you need to create a life you absolutely love is already inside of you. Sometimes harnessing that power will take you down paths you didn't expect (see note about falling on your face above), but when you choose to become deliberate and intentional about getting what you want, you will indeed create it.

So keep swimming. ***Don't stop believing.*** You've totally got this.

Oh, and don't worry about getting older. There's lots more Chardonnay and a lot less drama on this side of the fence.

It's actually quite fabulous.

AND SO ARE *You.*

ACKNOWLEDGEMENTS

Thank You to every mom in the Your Ideal Mom Life® and *Love Your Mom Life* communities. Thank you for showing up and tuning in week after week. You make these incredible communities what they are. And thank you for trusting me. I am humbled to be able to serve you.

....

Jo Dodd, you might not realize it, but you propelled me to make this book a reality. Thank you, friend. Your encouragement and support mean more to me than you know.

....

Thank you to Janica Smith at Publishing Smith and Kendra Cagle at 5 Lakes Design for taking this book from a file saved on Google Docs to the masterpiece it became. Your patience, support, and expertise were invaluable. I quite literally could not have published this book without you.

....

To everyone on Team Mascara, a hundred times, thank you! Yamiek Anthony, Kate Aquino, Kristy Baranovskis, Barbara Borges, Lara Costa, Donna DeSanctis, Jo Dodd, Rebecca Farmer, Nellie Harden, Yvonne Jimerson, Allyson Mancini, Ana Marin, Annie Mudin, Cameron Normand, Jessie Patterson, Stephanie Pletka, Marin Rankin, Megan Rempel, Leeann Rybakov, Lauren Schwarzfeld, Monica Sheffield, Jennie Stehli, Katie Straub, Yriana Torres, Jessica Velazquez, and Kendahl Yanez: Each of you stepped into your gifts to help me get this book out to the world. I will forever be grateful to each of you for helping me achieve a lifelong dream. You are supportive and loving beyond measure.

....

Rodger, Monica, Adam, Mommy, and Daddy, thank you for loving and believing in me always.

Lara, thank you for cheering me on and supporting me. And thank you for always telling me where the commas go.

....

Katie, Steph, and Amy, your love and support mean the world to me. Thank you for propping me up and calling me out; for giving me grace and telling me like it is; for being there and loving me unconditionally. You are, and always will be, my Celebration Circle.

....

Cameron, Yamiek, and Yvonne, I am so grateful to have found you on my business journey. You are more than an accountability group, you are true friends. I love you and can't thank you enough for supporting me as I've gone through the ups and downs of making my business what it is today.

....

Em and Ryan, I wrote this book for you. You two are the reason my heart is so full. I thank God every day that He chose me to be your mommy. You are my favorite kids in the whole world, and I love you more than you will ever know. Thanks for always believing in me and for giving me so much to write about.

....

And finally, thank you, Shawn. Thank you for loving me and cheering me on when I didn't believe I could do it. Thank you for challenging me and supporting me. You are my biggest cheerleader and my very best friend. I love you. You are my everything.

ABOUT THE AUTHOR

Nikki Oden is a lawyer and mom coach who helps working moms get unstuck by teaching them how to battle burnout, own their days, and lose the mom guilt. She is the founder of Your Ideal Mom Life® and host of the *Love Your Mom Life* podcast. Nikki's work has been featured in TODAY Parents, The Boston Globe, Cafe Mom, Thrive Global, Authority Magazine, Kidspot, and more.

Nikki is also an avid tennis player and aspiring sommelier. She resides in Palm Beach County, Florida, with her husband and two children.

Learn more by visiting **www.youridealmomlife.com** or connect with Nikki on Instagram (**@NikkiOden**).